DO ONE THING EVERY DAY TO CHANGE THE WORLD

A journal by:

_____

You cannot get through a single day without having an impact on the world around you. What you do makes a difference, and you have to decide what kind of difference you want to make.

Jane Goodall

This small book offers 365 ways to create positive change in the world. On its pages are inspiring quotes from naturalists, celebrities, politicians, and poets; stories of everyday role models ("Helping Hand"), from a hairstylist in the United States to a game warden in Rwanda; and disturbing facts about poverty, hunger, education, health, government, and the environment, with related actions that you can take now.

Some may look at the world's injustices, big and small, near and far, and shrug their shoulders at the enormity of the task. In this book, instead, you can flip through the undated pages to find ways to work at change, one day and one deed at a time.

In *Do One Thing Every Day to Change the World*, you will learn how long it takes aluminum cans (80 to 100 years) and plastic bottles (never!) to decompose, but also about recycling and upcycling and how to confront corporations about wasteful packaging. You will read about critically endangered animals, but also about days of action dedicated to them and protections that need to be better enforced. You will learn about the polluting of oceans, but also about people in India who cleaned up the mountains of trash on their seashore and saw the return of turtles missing for decades. You will find ways to contribute money or goods you have collected to organizations that will distribute them to causes that concern you. Finally you will discover through "self-tracking" how much you may be contributing to the world's problems with your own carbon emissions, food and water waste, or political indifference. You will also learn how to increase your positive impact on the world by what you eat, what you buy, how you live, and how you travel.

Whether you work on alleviating poverty, hunger, and disease throughout the world or on improving the life of a single needy person in your community, you are changing the world for the better. Thank you.

Note: To ensure that the facts cited are accurate and useful, their sources and dates were checked as close to publication as possible. Also, at the end of the book, for reference, is a Glossary of environmental terms.

DATE: __ / __ / __

Rate the difference you make for good in the world today (from 1 to 10, with 10 being the greatest): _____

Rate yourself again at the end of the book—after a year of doing one thing every day to change the world.

DATE: __/__/__

IN 2016, ONLY 56 PERCENT OF THE VOTING-AGE POPULATION WENT TO THE POLLS IN THE UNITED STATES TO CAST THEIR BALLOTS FOR PRESIDENT. OF THE 32 MOST HIGHLY DEVELOPED DEMOCRATIC COUNTRIES, THE UNITED STATES RANKED 26TH IN VOTER TURNOUT.

Pew Research Center

I: ☐ voted in the last presidential election

☐ did not vote in the last presidential election

☐ will vote in the next presidential election

DATE: __/__/__

CYCLE TRACKS WILL ABOUND IN UTOPIA.

H. G. Wells

☐ Today I made this new plan for riding my bicycle regularly:

_____

_____

_____

_____

_____

_____

_____

A TRUE CONSERVATIONIST KNOWS THAT THE WORLD IS NOT GIVEN BY HIS FATHERS, BUT BORROWED FROM HIS CHILDREN.

Unknown

When people put their ballots in the boxes, they are . . . inoculated against the feeling that the government is not theirs.

John Kenneth Galbraith

Today I: ☐ registered voters

☐ did something else to help get out the vote:

_____

_____

_____

_____

DATE: __ / __ / __

Bicycling 10 kilometers each way to work would save 1,500 kilograms of greenhouse gas emissions each year.

Department of Transport and Main Roads, Queensland, AU

Instead of driving from _____

to _____,

today I: ☐ rode my bike

☐ walked

☐ scootered

DATE: __ / __ / __

THE WORLD I INHERITED FROM MY FATHERS:

_____

_____

_____

_____

_____

_____

DATE: __ / __ / __

THE WORLD I WANT TO LEAVE FOR MY CHILDREN:

_____

_____

_____

_____

_____

_____

DATE: __ / __ / __

HELPING HAND

Todd Bol built the first Little Free Library in Hudson, Wisconsin, in 2009 as a tribute to his mother, a schoolteacher and an avid reader. It was a miniature schoolhouse (2 feet by 2 feet) mounted on a pole in his front yard and filled with books for neighbors to borrow and exchange. Now there are more than 75,000 of these mini libraries in 88 countries around the world. A nonprofit organization (littlefreelibrary.org) offers advice and even blueprints.

Todd Bol's story inspired me to:

_____

_____

_____

_____

_____

_____

KIDS READING AND PEOPLE READING TO THEM . . . CHANGES THE WHOLE ATTITUDE OF WHAT IS VALUED IN A COMMUNITY.

Todd Bol

Today I: ☐ read to a child at a community center

☐ exchanged some favorite books with friends

☐ started a Little Free Library

DATE: __ / __ / __

ANIMAL WATCH

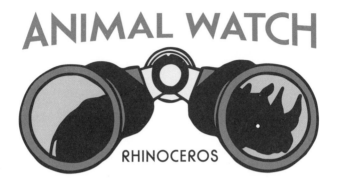

RHINOCEROS

One hundred years ago, about 500,000 wild rhinoceroses roamed Africa and Asia. Today fewer than 30,000 are left, living mostly in national parks and preserves. Poachers fetch high prices in Asia for rhinos' horns, which are mistakenly believed to have medicinal powers.

Today I: ☐ read more about rhinos

☐ marked World Rhino Day (September 22)
on my calendar as a day for action

No one in the world needs a Rhino horn but a Rhino.

Paul Oxton

☐ Today I vowed never to buy a product made of rhino horn and told others why.

DATE: __ / __ / __

Enough plastic is thrown away each year to circle the earth four times.

Recycling Coalition of Utah

Today I cut down on my use of plastic containers for:

☐ shopping

☐ drinking

☐ storage

TAKE ONLY PICTURES, LEAVE ONLY FOOTSTEPS.

Unknown

☐ Today I picked up trash from a park or a preserve.

OVERCOMING POVERTY IS NOT A GESTURE OF CHARITY. IT IS AN ACT OF JUSTICE.

Nelson Mandela

DATE: __ / __ / __

HOW I HELPED TO OVERCOME POVERTY IN MY COMMUNITY TODAY:

_____

_____

_____

_____

_____

_____

DATE: __ / __ / __

HOW I HELPED TO OVERCOME POVERTY IN THE WORLD TODAY:

_____

_____

_____

_____

_____

_____

DATE: __ / __ / __

One in six children who are not reading proficiently in third grade fail to graduate from high school on time.

The Annie E. Casey Foundation, 2012

☐ Today I volunteered to read with young children at an elementary school or another setting.

DATE: __ / __ / __

ASK ME MY THREE MAIN PRIORITIES FOR GOVERNMENT, AND I TELL YOU: EDUCATION, EDUCATION, AND EDUCATION.

Tony Blair

Today I helped _____ **apply**

☐ to a college

☐ to a training program

☐ for a scholarship

DATE: __ / __ / __

Community Service Day

Do one of these important services today. Check the box.

☐ Read to a blind person.

☐ Walk a shelter dog.

☐ Shop for an elderly neighbor.

☐ Collect toys/toiletries for a homeless shelter.

☐ Donate used clothes or furniture.

☐ Support veterans or military families.

☐ Be an English-conversation partner.

☐ Donate blood.

☐ Prepare taxes as a volunteer.

☐ Teach healthy cooking.

☐ Deliver meals to shut-ins.

☐ Welcome a new neighbor.

☐ Thank a firefighter, police officer, or veteran.

☐ _____
  something else

DATE: __ / __ / __

If you want others to be happy, practice compassion. If you want to be happy, practice compassion.

Dalai Lama

What I did for others today:

_____

_____

_____

_____

How I felt:

_____

_____

_____

_____

In 2015, 29 percent of the global population lacked safely managed drinking water supplies.

United Nations

☐ Today I organized a Water Challenge with friends. For two weeks we will drink only tap water and buy no beverages. We will donate the money saved to an organization such as thewaterproject.org, which creates reliable water projects in sub-Saharan Africa.

WHEN THE WELL'S DRY, WE KNOW THE WORTH OF WATER.

Benjamin Franklin

Today I: ☐ fixed _____ leaky faucets in my home

☐ saved water by:

_____

_____

_____

_____

ONE CHILD, ONE TEACHER, ONE BOOK, AND ONE PEN CAN CHANGE THE WORLD.

Malala Yousafzai

DATE: __ / __ / __

☐ TODAY I ARRANGED FOR MY WORKPLACE TO SPONSOR THIS SCHOOL:

_____

_____

_____

_____

_____

_____

DATE: __ / __ / __

☐ TODAY I HELPED RAISE MONEY FOR A SCHOOL LIBRARY BY:

_____

_____

_____

_____

_____

_____

DATE: __ / __ / __

The number of extremely poor people—those who live on $1.90 a day or less—is rising in sub-Saharan Africa. That region accounted for more than half of the extreme poor in 2015; by 2030 it is expected to be nearly 90 percent.

The World Bank

Today I: ☐ bought something from a company that donates all or part of its profits to a poverty-fighting charity

☐ bought a fair-trade and ethically sourced product from a craftsperson in a developing country

Philanthropy is commendable, but it must not cause the philanthropist to overlook the circumstances of economic injustice which make philanthropy necessary.

Martin Luther King Jr.

☐ Today I lent money through kiva.org or another microfinance organization for individuals or groups who want to invest in local products or start businesses.

CARBON FOOTPRINT CALCULATOR

Use the United States Environmental Protection Agency's Carbon Footprint Calculator (epa.gov/carbon-footprint -calculator) to rate the environmental cost of your home energy, transportation, and waste.

Home Energy Score: ☐ below average

☐ average

☐ above average

Transportation Score: ☐ below average

☐ average

☐ above average

Waste Score: ☐ below average

☐ average

☐ above average

DATE: __ / __ / __

We have forgotten how to be good guests, how to walk lightly on the earth as its other creatures do.

Barbara Ward Jackson and René Dubos

☐ Today I used this "planned action" from the EPA
(epa.gov/carbon-footprint-calculator) to reduce my carbon footprint:

_____

_____

_____

_____

_____

_____

DATE: __ / __ / __

Washing hands with soap and water prevents illnesses and the spread of infections to others. Global rates of handwashing after using the toilet are about 19 percent.

Centers for Disease Control and Prevention

Lather your hands with soap (back and front, under the nails, and between the fingers) and scrub for at least 20 seconds—the time it takes to hum "Happy Birthday" twice.

☐ Did it.

The awareness that health is dependent on habits that we control makes us the first generation in history that to a large extent determines its own destiny.

Jimmy Carter

Practice the "Dracula cough"—coughing or sneezing into your elbow—
to prevent spreading germs.

☐ Did it.

DATE: __ / __ / __

A SMALL GOOD DEED I DID TO BENEFIT MY COMMUNITY TODAY:

_____

_____

_____

_____

_____

_____

DATE: __ / __ / __

A SMALL GOOD DEED I DID TO BENEFIT THE WORLD TODAY:

_____

_____

_____

_____

_____

_____

How far that little candle throws his beams!

So shines a good deed in a naughty world.

William Shakespeare

OPTIMISM IS A MORAL CHOICE. I WAKE UP EVERY DAY AND CHOOSE TO BE OPTIMISTIC.

Chelsea Clinton

I am optimistic that this action I took today will make the world better:

_____

_____

_____

_____

_____

_____

PROBLEMS ARE ONLY OPPORTUNITIES IN WORK CLOTHES.

Henry J. Kaiser

Today's problem:

_____

_____

_____

My solution:

_____

_____

_____

HELPING HAND

Cacilda Fumo helps save hundreds of lives every year in Mozambique. Living with HIV, like 10 percent of the adults in her country, she first started a support group. Then she joined a program to make compliance with antiretroviral therapy easier by sending one group member on the long trip to pick up medicine for all. This led to organizing many more groups in her area. Now Fumo spends her days locating patients who have stopped treatment and persuading them to start again.

Cacilda Fumo's story inspired me to:

_____

_____

_____

_____

_____

We help people feel strong knowing they are not alone.

Cacilda Fumo

☐ Today I helped to support someone with this problem we have in
common:

_____

_____

_____

_____

_____

Ninety percent of the energy used by incandescent lightbulbs is wasted as heat. Switching to compact fluorescent bulbs or light-emitting diode bulbs will reduce the growth of energy demand and avoid carbon emissions.

US Department of Energy

☐ Today I changed _____ incandescent bulbs to fluorescents or LEDs.

DATE: __/__/__

SPARE A WATT;

SAVE A LOT.

Energy conservation slogan

Today I: ☐ consciously turned off the lights every time I left a room

☐ did something else to save energy:

_____

_____

_____

_____

_____

WHAT WOULD THE
WORLD BE, ONCE
BEREFT
    OF WET AND OF
    WILDNESS? LET
    THEM BE LEFT,
O LET THEM BE LEFT,
WILDNESS AND WET;
    LONG LIVE THE
    WEEDS AND THE
    WILDERNESS YET.

Gerard Manley Hopkins

DATE: __ / __ / __

A POND, A STREAM, OR AN OCEAN NEARBY THAT IS AT RISK:

_____

_____

TODAY I WILL HELP BY:

_____

_____

_____

DATE: __ / __ / __

AN AREA OF WILDERNESS NEARBY THAT IS AT RISK:

_____

_____

TODAY I WILL HELP BY:

_____

_____

_____

DATE: __ / __ / __

MAKE AMERICA KIND AGAIN.

▲
Slogan from the Women's March, 2017
▼

A kindness I did today:

_____

_____

_____

_____

_____

_____

_____

After playing Ruth [Bader Ginsburg], I realized how important it is to have a voice in the world.

Felicity Jones

A national issue I spoke up about today:

_____

_____

_____

_____

_____

_____

ANIMAL WATCH

SEA TURTLE

Nearly all species of sea turtle are classified as endangered. Poachers hunt them for their shells, skin, meat, and eggs. Climate change in some cases has altered the sand temperature for their nesting sites; warmer nests result in more females.

Today I: ☐ read more about sea turtles

☐ marked World Sea Turtle Day (June 16)

on my calendar as a day for action

The least movement is of importance to all nature. The entire ocean is affected by a pebble.

Blaise Pascal

☐ Today I vowed never to buy a product made from turtle shell and told others why.

DATE: __ / __ / __

By reducing your consumption of animal protein by half, you can cut your diet's carbon footprint by more than 40 percent.

BBC Future

WHY?

- As cows process food, they burp and pass gas, releasing methane (a greenhouse gas).

- Cows eat other possible sources of food, such as maize and soy.

- Raising cows requires water, fertilizer (which can release greenhouse gases), and land (which may be cleared of the trees that pull carbon dioxide, another greenhouse gas, from the air).

☐ **Today I cut my usual consumption of animal protein by half and committed to this as a permanent change in my diet.**

DATE: __ / __ / __

Nothing will benefit human health and increase the chances for survival of life on Earth as much as the evolution to a vegetarian diet.

Albert Einstein, attributed

My average weekly consumption of meat:

_____

_____

_____

_____

_____

Today I ate _____ instead of meat for dinner.

DATE: __ / __ / __

HOW I HELPED SOMEONE WHO WAS SUFFERING TODAY:

_____

_____

_____

DATE: __ / __ / __

HOW I HELPED SOMEONE WHO WAS HOMELESS TODAY:

_____

_____

_____

DATE: __ / __ / __

HOW I HELPED SOMEONE WHO WAS HUNGRY TODAY:

_____

_____

_____

Charity begins today. Today somebody is suffering, today somebody is in the street, today somebody is hungry. Our work is for today, yesterday has gone, tomorrow has not yet come. We have only today.

Mother Teresa

DATE: __ / __ / __

The odds of returning to prison were 43 percent lower for inmates who participated in correctional education programs than for those who did not.

RAND Corporation, 2013

Today I will: ☐ volunteer in a prison education program

☐ contact my congressional representatives and the Department of Justice to advocate for better educational opportunities in prisons

DATE: __ / __ / __

THERE IS NO SUCH THING AS FUNCTIONAL ILLITERACY . . . WHEN A PERSON IS ILLITERATE, HE IS NOT FUNCTIONAL.

Theodore Roosevelt, attributed

Today I:
☐ volunteered in an adult reading program

☐ helped an illiterate adult to find an adult reading program

DATE: __/__/__

DONATION DAY

CIVIL LIBERTIES

Today I researched these organizations through a nonprofit charity watch-dog organization, such as **Charity Navigator**, **CharityWatch**, or **GuideStar**.

- ☐ American Civil Liberties Union (ACLU)
- ☐ Center for Constitutional Rights
- ☐ Electronic Frontier Foundation
- ☐ Equal Justice Initiative
- ☐ National Urban League
- ☐ _____
  another organization

DATE: __ / __ / __

There is no greater joy in life than giving to worthy causes.

Ted Turner

Today I gave $_____ / _____
to this civil liberties organization:

_____

_____

goods/services

because:

_____

_____

_____

DATE: __/__/__

THE AVERAGE AMERICAN USES SEVEN TREES A YEAR IN PAPER, WOOD, AND OTHER PRODUCTS MADE FROM TREES. THIS AMOUNTS TO 2,000,000,000 TREES PER YEAR!

University of Southern Indiana

Today I: ☐ brought a ceramic mug to use at work instead of a paper cup

☐ did something else to reduce wasting paper:

_____

_____

_____

DATE: __ / __ / __

A CULTURE IS NO BETTER THAN ITS WOODS.

W. H. Auden

☐ Today I printed on both sides of the paper and recycled all my scrap paper.

IN A GENTLE WAY, YOU CAN SHAKE THE WORLD.

Mahatma Gandhi

DATE: __ / __ / __

HOW I GENTLY SHOOK MY LOCAL WORLD TODAY:

_____

_____

_____

_____

_____

_____

DATE: __ / __ / __

HOW I GENTLY SHOOK THE GLOBAL WORLD TODAY:

_____

_____

_____

_____

_____

_____

DATE: __ / __ / __

Nearly 34 million lawful immigrants live in the United States today.

Pew Research Center

Today I helped a new immigrant with: ☐ language

☐ food

☐ housing

☐ a job

☐ _____

other

GIVE ME YOUR TIRED,
YOUR POOR,
YOUR HUDDLED MASSES
YEARNING TO BREATHE FREE.

Emma Lazarus

☐ Today I volunteered at a refugee center.

Test Your Knowledge

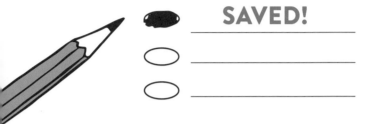

SAVED!

_____

_____

_____

Which animals below have been saved by conservationists?

- ☐ southern white rhinoceros
- ☐ panda bear
- ☐ Yellowstone grizzly bear
- ☐ gray wolf
- ☐ gray whale
- ☐ snow leopard
- ☐ northern brown kiwi

Answer: All of the above

If we can teach people about wildlife, they will be touched. Share my wildlife with me. Because humans want to save things that they love.

Steve Irwin

Today I shared my love of this animal:

_____

_____

_____

with:

_____

_____

_____

Cardiovascular diseases are the number one cause of death around the world, and 85 percent of these deaths are due to heart attack and stroke.

World Health Organization, 2017

☐ Today I learned CPR (cardiopulmonary resuscitation) through the American Red Cross or another organization.

HOPE FOR THE BEST AND PREPARE FOR THE WORST.

Seneca

☐ **Today I memorized the National Stroke Association's acronym for identifying the most common symptoms of a stroke (FAST):**

F—Face: Ask the person to smile. Does one side of the face droop?

A—Arms: Ask the person to raise both arms. Does one arm drift downward?

S—Speech: Ask the person to repeat a simple phrase. Is their speech slurred or strange?

T—Time: If you observe any of these signs, call 9-1-1 immediately.

DATE: __ / __ / __

HOW I HELPED SOMEONE TODAY BY DOING THIS HUMANITARIAN WORK:

_____

_____

_____

_____

_____

_____

DATE: __ / __ / __

HOW DOING THIS HUMANITARIAN WORK HELPED ME:

_____

_____

_____

_____

_____

THERE IS A MYTH
THAT THOSE WHO
DO HUMANITARIAN
WORK HAVE A
SAVIOR MENTALITY,
BUT THE RELATIONSHIP
IS RECIPROCAL.

Meghan Markle, *Duchess of Sussex*

DATE: __/__/__

You're either part of the solution or you're part of the problem.

Eldridge Cleaver

Problem:

_____

_____

_____

My solution:

_____

_____

_____

Our problems are man-made; therefore they can be solved by man.

John F. Kennedy

Problem:

_____

_____

_____

My solution:

_____

_____

_____

HELPING HAND

Erik Ahlström,
a Swedish skier and trail
runner, invented a combination
of jogging and environmentalism he calls "plogging"
(*plocka upp* is "pick up" in Swedish). As they run, ploggers fill
up bags with cans, bottles, paper, and other rubbish and then drop
them into garbage cans. In cities around the world, people of all ages
plog alone or find others online and through organized events.

Erik Ahlström's story inspired me to:

_____

_____

_____

_____

_____

_____

DATE: __ /__ /__

FOR YEARS I HAVE TRIED TO CHANGE
A BEHAVIOR THAT I THINK IS A SIGN
OF AN UNHEALTHY SOCIETY WITHOUT
RESPECT FOR EACH OTHER, AND THAT
IS LITTERING. THE SOLUTION IS SIMPLE.

Erik Ahlström

☐ Today I picked up litter on my block.

DATE: __ / __ / __

Revolving doors are both more efficient and more energy-efficient than swing doors. They move large numbers of people in and out of buildings while preventing hot air from escaping in winter and cold air in summer.

"Climate Fwd," *New York Times*

☐ Today I used _____ revolving doors instead of swing doors.
how many?

I do wonder whether there will come a time when we can no longer afford our wastefulness.

John Steinbeck

☐ On this hot day I raised my household thermostat to

_____ degrees Fahrenheit.

☐ On this cold day I lowered my household thermostat to

_____ degrees Fahrenheit.

THE DIFFERENCE BETWEEN MAN'S SOOT AND NATURE'S GRIME IS THAT NATURE KNOWS HOW TO CLEAN UP AFTER HERSELF.

Stanford Research Institute

DATE: __ / __ / __

HOW I CLEANED UP MY SOOT TODAY:

_____

_____

_____

_____

_____

_____

DATE: __ / __ / __

HOW I AVOIDED CREATING SOOT TODAY:

_____

_____

_____

_____

_____

The 116th US Congress was the most diverse ever. A record 106 women serve in the House, and there are more women of color and LGBT members now.

Candidates I supported in the most recent election:

_____

_____

_____

_____

_____

DATE: __ / __ / __

ALL POLITICS IS LOCAL.

Tip O'Neill

Today I: ☐ worked for _____ , a great local candidate

☐ did something else in community politics:

_____

_____

_____

_____

_____

DATE: __ / __ / __

ANIMAL WATCH

GORILLA

The population of gorillas has been declining for decades. Their survival is threatened by civil conflicts in Africa, poaching, disease, and the clearing of their forest habitats for farming and livestock. One hopeful sign, however, is that due to conservation efforts, the mountain gorilla population grew from 620 in 1989 to more than 1,000 now.

Today I: ☐ read more about gorillas

☐ marked World Gorilla Day (September 24)

on my calendar as a day for action

DATE: __ / __ / __

Mankind's true moral test, its fundamental test (which lies deeply buried from view), consists of its attitude towards those who are at its mercy: animals.

Milan Kundera

Today I: ☐ joined an animal conservation organization

☐ did something else for animals:

_____

_____

_____

DATE: __/__/__

Personal vehicles generate around 30 million tons of CO_2 every year just by idling—running the engine when the car is not moving.

US Department of Energy

Today I: ☐ limited idling time in my car to less than 10 seconds

☐ told someone with a car the consequences of idling

DATE: __/__/__

CLEAR THE AIR!
CLEAN THE SKY!
WASH THE WIND!

T. S. Eliot

☐ Today I bought food grown locally rather than trucked over long distances.

DATE: __ / __ / __

A HOPEFUL SOLUTION TO A WORLD PROBLEM I LEARNED ABOUT TODAY:

_____

_____

_____

_____

_____

_____

DATE: __ / __ / __

HOW I CAN CONTRIBUTE TO SOLVING A WORLD PROBLEM:

_____

_____

_____

_____

_____

_____

Although
the world is
full of suffering,
it is full also of
the overcoming
of it.

Helen Keller

EDUCATION IS THE MOST POWERFUL WEAPON WHICH YOU CAN USE TO CHANGE THE WORLD.

Nelson Mandela

☐ Today I educated someone about:

_____

_____

_____

_____

_____

_____

DATE: __ / __ / __

Fifty-nine million children of primary school age are being denied an education, and almost 65 million adolescents are without access to a secondary school. Conflict and natural disasters have disrupted the education of 75 million children.

Global Citizen

☐ Today I donated money or volunteered my services to an international charity for children's education.

DATE: __ / __ / __

Community Service Day

**Do one of these important
services today. Check the box.**

☐ Read to a blind person.

☐ Walk a shelter dog.

☐ Shop for an elderly neighbor.

☐ Collect toys/toiletries for a
homeless shelter.

☐ Donate used clothes or furniture.

☐ Support veterans or military
families.

☐ Be an English-conversation
partner.

☐ Donate blood.

☐ Prepare taxes as a volunteer.

☐ Teach healthy cooking.

☐ Deliver meals to shut-ins.

☐ Welcome a new neighbor.

☐ Thank a firefighter, police officer,
or veteran.

☐ _____
something else

Nothing is more beautiful than cheerfulness in an old face.

Johann Paul Friedrich Richter

Today I: ☐ helped out at a nursing home

☐ did this act of kindness for an elderly or frail person:

_____

_____

_____

_____

_____

_____

_____

DATE: __ / __ / __

NO MATTER HOW REMOTE WE FEEL WE ARE FROM THE OCEANS, EVERY ACT EACH ONE OF US TAKES IN OUR EVERYDAY LIVES AFFECTS OUR PLANET'S WATER CYCLE AND IN RETURN AFFECTS US.

Fabien Cousteau

☐ Today I chose environmentally safe cleaning liquids to avoid adding toxins to the water.

DATE: __ / __ / __

Of the estimated **29** billion gallons
of water used daily by US households,
nearly **30** percent is for outdoor use.
In the hot summer months or in dry
climates, this can rise to **70** percent.

▲
**United States Environmental
Protection Agency**
▼

**Today I started making my yard a water-smart landscape or told others
how to do it by:**

☐ planting low-water-use native plants suitable to the region and the site

☐ grouping plants with similar water needs together

☐ planting water-guzzling turf grass only where necessary

☐ avoiding steep slopes or using plants with deep roots to prevent
erosion and runoff

Man is the only animal that laughs and weeps; for he is the only animal that is struck with the difference between what things are, and what they ought to be.

William Hazlitt

DATE: __/__/__

WHAT THE GOVERNMENT IS TODAY:

_____

_____

_____

_____

_____

_____

DATE: __/__/__

WHAT THE GOVERNMENT SHOULD BE TODAY:

_____

_____

_____

_____

_____

_____

THE HUNGER OF ONE IS THE SHAME OF ALL.

African proverb

Today I: ☐ put aside a jar for loose change to donate to the hungry

☐ set up another regular plan for giving

DATE: __ / __ / __

IN 2016, AN ESTIMATED 12.3 PERCENT OF AMERICAN HOUSEHOLDS WERE "FOOD INSECURE" AT LEAST SOME OF THE TIME DURING THE YEAR. THIS MEANS THAT THEY LACKED ACCESS TO ENOUGH FOOD FOR AN ACTIVE, HEALTHY LIFE FOR ALL HOUSEHOLD MEMBERS.

US Department of Agriculture

Today I: ☐ collected food for a food bank

☐ served at a soup kitchen

CITIZENSHIP

How active are you as a local, national, and world citizen?

Local

☐ attend local political meetings

☐ work to elect candidates whose ideas I support

☐ vote in primaries ☐ vote in general elections

National

☐ keep informed about national issues

☐ work to elect candidates whose ideas I support

☐ vote in primaries ☐ vote in general elections

World

☐ learn about world issues

☐ contact national leaders about my views

☐ join organizations that influence world affairs

Rate yourself as a citizen (from 1 to 10, with 10 being the greatest):

Local_____; National_____; World _____

DATE: __/__/__

DEMOCRACY IS NOT ABOUT WORDS, BUT ACTION.

Eleanor Roosevelt

A political action I took today:

_____

_____

_____

_____

_____

_____

Vaccinations prevent between 2 million and 3 million deaths every year.

World Health Organization

Today I: ☐ volunteered at a clinic where vaccinations are given

☐ lobbied elected officials to support vaccination efforts

in the United States and around the world

AN OUNCE OF PREVENTION IS WORTH A POUND OF CURE.

American proverb

Today I: ☐ made sure that my vaccinations are up to date

☐ made sure that my family's vaccinations are up to date

DATE: __ / __ / __

WHEN I WILL HELP A NEEDY PERSON:

_____

_____

_____

_____

_____

_____

DATE: __ / __ / __

WHERE I WILL HELP A NEEDY PERSON:

_____

_____

_____

_____

_____

_____

The primary questions for an adult are not *why* or *how,* but *when* and *where.*

Eugen Rosenstock-Huessy

DATE: __/__/__

It's the little things citizens do. That's what will make the difference. My little thing is planting trees.

Wangari Maathai

The little thing I did today that will make a difference:

_____

_____

_____

_____

_____

_____

_____

DATE: __ / __ / __

That best portion of a good man's life,

His little, nameless, unremembered acts

Of kindness and of love.

William Wordsworth

My little act of kindness and love today:

_____

_____

_____

_____

_____

_____

HELPING HAND

In college, Maria Rose Belding started a free online platform for connecting businesses that had extra food, such as grocery stores and restaurants, to nearby soup kitchens, homeless shelters, and food pantries. Since 2015 her nonprofit, MEANS (Matching Excess and Need for Stability; meansdatabase.org), has redistributed more than 1.8 million pounds of food and now has more than 3,000 partners nationwide.

Maria Rose Belding's story inspired me to:

_____

_____

_____

_____

_____

_____

DATE: __ / __ / __

I'm definitely not having a normal college experience. I've never been to a Greek life event, I'm not in any clubs, and I know I would have a much better GPA if I wasn't doing this [redistributing food]. But this is more important than me.

Maria Rose Belding

This is more important than me:

_____

_____

_____

Today I matched _____ 's

excess ☐ food ☐ clothing ☐ furniture ☐ _____

with _____, who needed it.

The **ENERGY STAR** label was created by the US government to identify products that use energy efficiently. Its goal is to reduce greenhouse gas emissions and other pollutants as well as to lower energy bills for consumers and businesses. Since its start in 1992, the program has helped save nearly 4 trillion kilowatt-hours of electricity and $450 billion.

☐ Today I commit to buying only **ENERGY STAR** products.

DATE: __/__/__

look for

WaterSense

· Meets EPA Criteria ·

The **WaterSense** label indicates products that meet the Environmental Protection Agency's criteria for efficiency and performance. These products must not only use at least 20 percent less water than standard models and save energy but also perform equally well.

☐ Today I commit to buying only WaterSense products.

Whenever we do what we can, we immediately can do more.

James Freeman Clarke

DATE: __ / __ / __

SOMETHING I COULD AND DID DO TODAY TO HELP THE ENVIRONMENT:

_____

_____

_____

_____

_____

_____

DATE: __ / __ / __

SOMETHING MORE I CAN DO NOW TO HELP THE ENVIRONMENT:

_____

_____

_____

_____

_____

_____

In 2017, women in the United States were paid just 80 percent of what men were paid, and that figure is even lower for many women of color. The gender pay gap refers to the median annual pay of all women who work full-time and year-round, compared with the pay of a similar cohort of men.

American Association of University Women

☐ Today I will find out how strong my state's equal pay laws are.

DATE: __ / __ / __

I do not demand equal pay for any women save those who do equal work in value.

Susan B. Anthony

☐ Today I will lobby my state and congressional representatives to make equal pay legislation national.

ANIMAL WATCH

PANDA

Pandas live mainly in forests in the mountains of western China and eat bamboo. They are crucial to the survival of the forests, because they spread seeds and aid in the growth of vegetation. Poaching by humans and deforestation have left just over 1,800 pandas in the wild. The Chinese government has established more than 50 panda reserves, but they protect only 61 percent of the country's pandas.

☐ Today I marked National Panda Day (March 16) on my calendar as a day for action.

KNOWING SOMEONE WHO BELONGS TO ANOTHER SPECIES CAN ENLARGE YOUR SOUL IN SURPRISING WAYS.

Sy Montgomery

☐ Today I read more about the plight of pandas and plan
   to educate others.

DATE: __ / __ / __

Aircraft account for 12 percent of all US transportation greenhouse gas emissions and 3 percent of total US greenhouse gas emissions.

United States Environmental Protection Agency

Today I will: ☐ plan fewer airplane trips, burning less jet fuel

☐ drive short distances rather than fly

DATE: __ / __ / __

IN NATURE THERE ARE NEITHER REWARDS NOR PUNISHMENTS— THERE ARE CONSEQUENCES.

Robert G. Ingersoll

When I fly, I will take these measures to reduce the negative consequences for nature:

☐ fly nonstop, since about 25 percent of emissions come from landing and taking off

☐ fly coach, since more passengers travel on the same amount of fuel

☐ buy carbon offsets that support tree planting and wind farms, for example, from airlines that offer them

MORAL COURAGE—
NOT AFRAID TO
SAY OR DO WHAT
YOU BELIEVE
TO BE RIGHT.

Bernard Law Montgomery

DATE: __ / __ / __

WHAT I SAID THAT I BELIEVE TO BE RIGHT TODAY:

_____

_____

_____

_____

_____

_____

DATE: __ / __ / __

WHAT I DID THAT I BELIEVE TO BE RIGHT TODAY:

_____

_____

_____

_____

_____

_____

DATE: __ / __ / __

Women hold 47 percent of all US jobs but only 24 percent of STEM (science, technology, engineering, math) jobs.

US Department of Commerce

☐ Today I marked International Day of Women and Girls in Science (February 11) on my calendar as a day for action.

Being a woman scientist in my country [Ghana] is very challenging. . . . When I am out in the field collecting data, some people . . . wonder why a woman is in a forest with a team of men. But I love what I do, and all of these challenges encourage me to learn and do more as a woman scientist.

Adwoba Kua-Manza Edjah

☐ Today I mentored _____ in a STEM field or helped her find someone who could.

DATE: __/__/__

DONATION DAY

CHILD WELFARE

Today I researched these organizations through a nonprofit charity watchdog organization, such as **Charity Navigator**, **CharityWatch**, or **GuideStar**:

- ☐ Child Find of America, Inc.
- ☐ Children International
- ☐ Prevent Child Abuse America
- ☐ Save the Children
- ☐ Unbound
- ☐ _____
  another organization

Liberality is not giving largely but giving wisely.

Proverb

Today I gave $_____ / _____
                                                        goods/services
to this child welfare organization:

_____

_____

because:

_____

_____

_____

PLANETARY

An international team of scientists has developed a daily food allotment for adults to improve health, feed the population of 10 billion expected by 2050, and save the planet by ensuring sustainable food.

The Lancet, 2019

Vegetables: 300 grams/10.6 ounces _____

Dairy: 250 grams/8.8 ounces _____

Whole Grains: 232 grams/8.2 ounces _____

Fruits: 200 grams/7 ounces _____

Legumes: 75 grams/2.6 ounces _____

Added fats: 51.8 grams/1.8 ounces _____

Starchy vegetables: 50 grams/1.8 ounces _____

Nuts: 50 grams/1.8 ounces _____

Added sugars: 31 grams/1.1 ounces _____

Poultry: 29 grams/1 ounce _____

Fish: 28 grams/1 ounce _____

Eggs: 13 grams/0.5 ounce _____

Beef and lamb: 7 grams/0.2 ounce _____

Pork: 7 grams/0.2 ounce _____

HEALTH DIET

DATE: __ / __ / __

FILL IN THE BLANKS OPPOSITE TO COMPARE YOUR DAILY DIET WITH THE
PLANETARY HEALTH DIET.

DATE: __ / __ / __

TODAY I WILL MAKE THESE CHANGES TO MY DIET:

_____

_____

_____

_____

_____

_____

_____

_____

DATE: __ / __ / __

HOW I STOPPED ONE HEART FROM BREAKING TODAY:

_____

_____

_____

_____

_____

_____

DATE: __ / __ / __

HOW I EASED ONE LIFE THE ACHING TODAY:

_____

_____

_____

_____

_____

_____

If I can stop one heart
from breaking,
I shall not live in vain;
If I can ease one life
the aching,
Or cool one pain,
Or help one fainting robin
Unto his nest again,
I shall not live in vain.

Emily Dickinson

DATE: __ / __ / __

We help support the type of world we want when we spend money on groceries, our car, and our clothes. . . . Today's growing supply chain transparency really empowers us to find out if the human beings who sewed those jeans or picked those tomatoes were employed ethically, or not.

▲
Jane Mosbacher Morris
▼

☐ Today I researched this purchase through KnowTheChain.org:

_____

_____

_____

_____

_____

_____

DATE: __ / __ / __

BUY LESS, CHOOSE WELL.

Vivienne Westwood

☐ Today I chose this purchase well, with the good of the world in mind:

_____

_____

_____

_____

_____

_____

_____

Test Your Knowledge

SAVING WATER

_____

_____

Estimate how many gallons it takes to:

flush a toilet: _____

take a five-minute shower: _____

take a bath: _____

brush your teeth with the water running: _____

shave with the water running: _____

run the dishwasher: _____

wash dishes by hand: _____

Answers: 2–7; 15–25; 70; 4; 10; 9–12; 9–20

DATE: __ / __ / __

All the water that will ever be is, right now.

National Geographic, 1993

Today I saved _____ water by:

how much?

_____

_____

_____

_____

_____

_____

DATE: __/__/__

EVERY DAY, MORE THAN 130 PEOPLE IN THE UNITED STATES DIE AFTER OVERDOSING ON OPIOIDS.

National Institute on Drug Abuse

☐ Today I disposed of my unused, expired, or unwanted medicines safely
so that they will not be ingested accidentally or misused intentionally.
(For details, see "Safe Disposal of Medicines" at www.fda.gov.)

DATE: __/__/__

ADDICTION IS THE NUMBER ONE DISEASE IN OUR CIVILIZATION.

Deepak Chopra

☐ If there are opioids in my house, I will have Narcan on hand and know how to use it.

IT ALWAYS SEEMS IMPOSSIBLE UNTIL IT IS DONE.

Nelson Mandela, attributed

DATE: __ / __ / __

THIS SEEMS LIKE AN IMPOSSIBLE GOAL:

_____

_____

_____

_____

_____

_____

DATE: __ / __ / __

AN "IMPOSSIBLE" GOAL THAT I ACHIEVED TODAY:

_____

_____

_____

_____

_____

_____

No person was ever honored for what he received. Honor has been the reward for what he gave.

Calvin Coolidge

Something I gave today:

_____

_____

_____

_____

_____

_____

_____

BEHOLD, I DO NOT GIVE LECTURES OR A LITTLE CHARITY, WHEN I GIVE I GIVE MYSELF.

Walt Whitman

How I gave of myself today:

_____

_____

_____

_____

_____

_____

HELPING HAND

Abisoye Ajayi-
Akinfolarin gave up
a successful technology career
in Lagos, Nigeria, to start GirlsCoding (girlscoding.com.ng),
a free program that teaches girls about computer programming.
She had noticed how few women were in her field and wanted to close
the gender gap by teaching disadvantaged girls how to code, design,
and build websites. The organization has trained more than
400 young Nigerian women to code since 2012.

Abisoye Ajayi-Akinfolarin's story inspired me to:

_____

_____

_____

_____

_____

_____

One thing I want my girls to hold on to is, regardless of where they are coming from, they can make it. They are coders. They are thinkers. Their future is bright.

Abisoye Ajayi-Akinfolarin

☐ Today I will encourage a girl to enter the computer field.

DATE: __/__/__

If each American replaced chicken with plant-based foods at just one meal per week, the carbon dioxide savings would be the same as taking more than half a million cars off the road.

Environmental Defense Fund

☐ Today I will plan a plant-based meal to replace one chicken dinner this week.

People try to do all sorts of clever and difficult things to improve life instead of doing the simplest, easiest thing—refusing to participate in activities that make life bad.

Leo Tolstoy

Today I will:

- ☐ refuse to eat livestock
- ☐ refuse to use a plastic bag
- ☐ refuse to drive without a full car

DATE: __ / __ / __

SOMETHING I WOULD LIKE TO HAPPEN TO IMPROVE THE WORLD TODAY:

_____

_____

_____

_____

_____

_____

DATE: __ / __ / __

SOMETHING I MADE HAPPEN TO IMPROVE THE WORLD TODAY:

_____

_____

_____

_____

_____

_____

I like things
to happen,
and if they
don't happen
I like to make
them happen.

Winston Churchill

If you want to be an empowered citizen in our democracy, able not only to navigate society and its institutions, but also to improve and shape them, you need to thoroughly understand how the US Constitution works.

College Board, 2017

☐ Today I will reread the US Constitution to figure out how I can use it to ensure voting rights for all.

DATE: __ / __ / __

If you want to be an empowered and adaptive worker or artist or writer or scientist or teacher, and be able to shape the world around you, you need to know how computers work and how to use them.

College Board, 2017

Today I will: ☐ start to improve my computer skills in order to be effective

☐ help others improve their computer skills

ANIMAL WATCH

PENGUIN

The penguins that live in Antarctica depend on sea ice for access to food and for places to breed. With global warming, that ice has been disappearing along with the penguin population.

Today I: ☐ read more about penguins

☐ marked World Penguin Day (April 25) on my calendar as a day for action

DATE: __ / __ / __

The question is not, Can they [animals] reason? nor, Can they talk? but, Can they suffer?

Jeremy Bentham

☐ Today I took this action to protect penguins and their environment:

_____

_____

_____

_____

SWAPS FOR A SUSTAINABLE BATHROOM

Mark **X** for what you already do and **Y** for what you plan to do in the future.

- ☐ Use a shampoo bar instead of a shampoo bottle.
- ☐ Use apple cider vinegar for conditioner instead of a commercial product.
- ☐ Use a safety razor instead of disposable razors.
- ☐ Use a bar of soap instead of body wash.
- ☐ Use a bamboo toothbrush instead of a plastic one.
- ☐ Use paper-wrapped toilet paper with recycled content instead of plastic-wrapped soft tissues made from trees.
- ☐ Use a sage bundle instead of an air freshener.
- ☐ Use silk thread to floss instead of plasticized thread.

DATE: __/__/__

IT IS THE GREATEST OF ALL MISTAKES TO DO NOTHING BECAUSE YOU CAN ONLY DO LITTLE. DO WHAT YOU CAN.

Sydney Smith

☐ Today I took this little action to make a sustainable bathroom:

_____

_____

_____

_____

_____

_____

_____

DATE: __ / __ / __

What counts is not necessarily the size of the dog in the fight—it's the size of the fight in the dog.

Dwight D. Eisenhower

☐ Today I fought fiercely for this cause on my own:

_____

_____

_____

_____

_____

_____

When spider webs unite, they can tie up a lion.

Ethiopian proverb

☐ Today I participated in this group action:

_____

_____

_____

_____

_____

_____

_____

DATE: __/__/__

A child whose mother can read is 50 percent more likely to survive past the age of five.

Global Citizen

☐ Today I donated or volunteered my services to an international charity for adult literacy.

EDUCATION . . . IS THE GREAT EQUALIZER OF THE CONDITIONS OF MEN,–THE BALANCE WHEEL OF SOCIAL MACHINERY.

Horace Mann

☐ Today I volunteered in an early-intervention reading program at a day care center, preschool, or library.

DATE: __/__/__

Community Service Day

Do one of these important services today. Check the box.

- ☐ Read to a blind person.
- ☐ Walk a shelter dog.
- ☐ Shop for an elderly neighbor.
- ☐ Collect toys/toiletries for a homeless shelter.
- ☐ Donate used clothes or furniture.
- ☐ Support veterans or military families.
- ☐ Be an English-conversation partner.

- ☐ Donate blood.
- ☐ Prepare taxes as a volunteer.
- ☐ Teach healthy cooking.
- ☐ Deliver meals to shut-ins.
- ☐ Welcome a new neighbor.
- ☐ Thank a firefighter, police officer, or veteran.
- ☐ _____
  something else

DATE: __ / __ / __

IF YOU SEE SOMEONE WITHOUT A SMILE, GIVE 'EM YOURS.

Dolly Parton

☐ Today I smiled at _____.

DATE: __ / __ / __

According to a UN study, **44.7 million tons** of e-waste (electronics) was discarded in **2016**, and only **20 percent** of it was handled properly. Yet some of the materials in these products, such as plastics, glass, and metal, can be recycled. Others are toxic, such as lead, mercury, and cadmium, and need to be disposed of carefully.

Consumer Reports

Today I will: ☐ bring my unused electronics to a recycling center

☐ donate them to a charity or nonprofit

☐ take them to a tech firm to dispose of responsibly

DATE: __ / __ / __

WE ARE LIVING ON THIS PLANET AS IF WE HAD ANOTHER ONE TO GO TO.

Terri Swearingen

Today I: ☐ got an electronic device repaired rather than disposing of it

☐ found a new home for a device I no longer use

DATE: __ / __ / __

I HAVE HOPE THAT I CAN IMPROVE THE WORLD IN THIS WAY:

_____

_____

_____

_____

_____

_____

DATE: __ / __ / __

I HAVE HOPE THAT I CAN IMPROVE MY COMMUNITY IN THIS WAY:

_____

_____

_____

_____

_____

_____

HOPE,
THE BEST
COMFORT
OF OUR
IMPERFECT
CONDITION.

Edward Gibbon

DATE: __ / __ / __

In 2017, more than one in eight Americans was considered officially poor; of those, almost one-third were children.

Poverty Solutions, University of Michigan

☐ Today I will do this to help poor people in my community:

_____

_____

_____

_____

_____

_____

_____

DATE: __ / __ / __

We cannot exist as a little island of well-being in a world where two-thirds of the people go to bed hungry every night.

Eleanor Roosevelt

☐ Today I will take this action to alleviate hunger:

_____

_____

_____

_____

_____

_____

_____

DATE: __/__/__

WATER FOOTPRINT CALCULATOR

Use the Water Footprint Calculator (watercalculator.org) to rate the environmental cost of your indoor, outdoor, and virtual water use.

Indoor Water Use: ☐ below average
☐ average
☐ above average

Outdoor Water Use: ☐ below average
☐ average
☐ above average

Virtual* Water Use: ☐ below average
☐ average
☐ above average

This includes all the water used in the steps to make a product.

DATE: __ / __ / __

No ocean, no life.
No blue, no green.

Sylvia Earle

Today I used this tip from the Water Footprint Calculator
(watercalculator.org) to reduce my water footprint:

_____

_____

_____

_____

_____

_____

_____

_____

DATE: __ / __ / __

EVERY DAY, 100 AMERICANS ARE KILLED WITH GUNS.

Centers for Disease Control and Prevention

Today I: ☐ made sure that my guns are stored safely at home

☐ lobbied my state and congressional representatives for stronger gun laws

Any way you cut it, one of the biggest threats to life as a teen in the US today is being shot.

Emma Gonzalez

Today I: ☐ joined an organization that lobbies for stronger gun laws

☐ educated others about the dangers of unregulated gun sales

DATE: __ / __ / __

I WORE OUT MY SHOES CAMPAIGNING FOR THIS CANDIDATE TODAY:

_____

_____

_____

_____

_____

_____

DATE: __ / __ / __

I WORE OUT MY SHOES CAMPAIGNING FOR THIS CAUSE TODAY:

_____

_____

_____

_____

_____

_____

It is better to wear out one's shoes than one's sheets.

Genoese proverb

LIFE IS TOO SHORT TO BE SMALL.

Benjamin Disraeli, attributed

DATE: __ / __ / __

A LARGE GESTURE I MADE TO PROTECT THE ENVIRONMENT TODAY:

_____

_____

_____

_____

_____

_____

DATE: __ / __ / __

A LARGE GESTURE I MADE TO RELIEVE POVERTY TODAY:

_____

_____

_____

_____

_____

_____

HELPING HAND

In 2015, Afroz Shah, a young Indian lawyer, started picking up garbage by hand from Versova Beach in Mumbai. The 2.5-kilometer stretch was covered with rotting litter, many feet high in places. He recruited local residents to his weekend cleanups and taught them sustainable waste practices. Shah and his team of volunteers have picked up 4,000 tons of garbage. Recently, turtle hatchlings from a vulnerable species returned for the first time in decades.

Afroz Shah's story inspired me to:

_____

_____

_____

_____

_____

_____

I AM AN OCEAN LOVER AND FEEL THAT WE OWE A DUTY TO OUR OCEAN TO MAKE IT FREE OF PLASTIC.

Afroz Shah

I am an ocean lover, and today I feel that my duty to the ocean is:

_____

_____

_____

_____

_____

_____

DATE: __/__/__

FOR THE PRICE OF A DAILY CAPPUCCINO FOR A WEEK, YOU CAN:

- buy a flock of ducks, chicks, or geese for a family in Bangladesh or Cambodia (Heifer International)
- provide 250 meals to families in need (Feeding America)
- contribute to a microsavings program that empowers women (CARE)
- send mosquito nets to families in Africa and other malaria-prone areas (Save the Children)
- buy water dishes, a leash, and a collar for a guide dog (Guide Dog Foundation)
- pay for emergency care for a malnourished child (International Rescue Committee)

This week, instead of drinking cappuccinos, I will:

_____

_____

_____

_____

DATE: __/__/__

BE CHARITABLE AND INDULGENT TO EVERYONE BUT THYSELF.

Joseph Joubert, attributed

☐ Today I gave up _____ for a week and donated
                        personal indulgence

the money to _____.

DATE: __ / __ / __

WHAT I DID TO IMPROVE SANITATION IN THE WORLD TODAY:

_____

_____

_____

_____

_____

_____

DATE: __ / __ / __

WHAT I DID TO IMPROVE EDUCATION IN THE WORLD TODAY:

_____

_____

_____

_____

_____

_____

Soap and education are not as sudden as a massacre, but they are more deadly in the long run.

Mark Twain

DATE: __ / __ / __

Sample Letter to a Corporate Polluter

Dear [president of company],

I have been a loyal customer of yours for more than _____ years and hoped to remain so for many years to come. I have also, in the past, given [your product] the highest ratings on Internet sales sites.

I have come to be a fervent believer in zero waste, however. This means rejecting single-use products, reusing goods, and diverting trash from landfills so that plastic does not increasingly pollute our land and waters. Unfortunately, because of its wasteful packaging, [your product] does not meet this standard, and I will no longer purchase it.

I look forward to changes in your packaging policy and to becoming a customer again.

Sincerely,

_____

☐ Today I wrote a letter like the sample to _____.

DATE: __/__/__

Whatever little we have gained, we have gained by agitation, while we have uniformly lost by moderation.

Daniel O'Connell

_____ is harming the environment this way:
local polluter

_____.

Today I agitated against the polluter by:

☐ writing a letter

☐ collecting signatures on a petition

☐ filing a complaint with a local official or agency

☐ organizing a boycott

☐ _____
other

ANIMAL WATCH

ELEPHANT

Elephants risk being killed for their ivory tusks, and their numbers dramatically decreased in the 20th century. Despite a ban in 1989 on the international trade of ivory, there are still some thriving and unregulated domestic markets.

Today I: ☐ read more about elephants

☐ marked World Elephant Day (August 12) on my calendar as a day for action

DATE: __/__/__

Nature's great masterpiece, an elephant, The only harmless great thing.

John Donne

Today I: ☐ supported an ivory crush or burn

☐ vowed not to buy anything made of elephant ivory
and told others why

Annually 18.7 million acres of forests are lost from fires, clear-cutting for agriculture and development, unsustainable logging, and other causes. Deforestation threatens people's livelihoods and a wide range of plants and animals, especially in tropical rain forests. Since trees soak up carbon dioxide, deforestation also accounts for about 15 percent of all greenhouse gas emissions.

World Wildlife Fund

☐ Today I joined an organization that works to save and restore forests.

DATE: __/__/__

WOODMAN, SPARE
THAT TREE!
TOUCH NOT
A SINGLE BOUGH!
IN YOUTH IT SHELTERED ME,
AND I'LL PROTECT IT NOW.

George Pope Morris

☐ Today I helped to plant or care for trees in my community.

HE WHO DOES ANYTHING BECAUSE IT IS THE CUSTOM, MAKES NO CHOICE.

John Stuart Mill

DATE: __ / __ / __

A NEW POLITICAL CAUSE I CHOSE TO SUPPORT TODAY:

_____

_____

_____

_____

_____

_____

DATE: __ / __ / __

A NEW CHARITY I CHOSE TO SUPPORT TODAY:

_____

_____

_____

_____

_____

_____

Why are more than 130 million girls out of school?

Malala Fund

- ☐ child labor
- ☐ early marriage
- ☐ wars
- ☐ cost
- ☐ gender bias
- ☐ health
- ☐ natural disasters
- ☐ poor quality
- ☐ all of the above

Answer: All of the above

I am here to speak up for the right of education of every child.

Malala Yousafzai

☐ Today I supported a school for disadvantaged girls in a developing country or an area of conflict.

DATE: __ / __ / __

DONATION DAY

ENVIRONMENT

Today I researched these organizations through a nonprofit charity watch-dog organization, such as **Charity Navigator, CharityWatch, or GuideStar.**

- ☐ Earthworks
- ☐ National Park Foundation
- ☐ Sierra Club Foundation
- ☐ Water.org
- ☐ World Resources Institute
- ☐ _____

another organization

DATE: __ / __ / __

The rich man is not one who is in possession of much, but one who gives much.

Saint John Chrysostom

Today I gave $_____ / _____

to this environmental organization:

goods/services

_____

_____

because:

_____

_____

_____

DATE: __/__/__

The United States has one of the largest wealth inequality gaps in the world. The wealthiest 1 percent of households in America own more than 40 percent of the nation's wealth. In recent decades this gap has gotten even wider. The vast inequality is bad for the American economy and even more detrimental to poor households with no upward mobility.

The Borgen Project

☐ Today I will work for legislation to close the wealth inequality gap in the United States.

If a free society cannot help the many who are poor, it cannot save the few who are rich.

John F. Kennedy

☐ Today I will fulfill my responsibility to the poor by:

_____

_____

_____

_____

_____

The time is always right to do right.

Martin Luther King Jr.

DATE: __ / __ / __

TODAY THE TIME IS RIGHT TO DO SOMETHING ABOUT HEALTH:

_____

_____

_____

_____

_____

_____

DATE: __ / __ / __

TODAY THE TIME IS RIGHT TO DO SOMETHING ABOUT POVERTY:

_____

_____

_____

_____

_____

_____

BY 2050, IF WE REMAIN ON THE CURRENT TRACK, OCEANS WILL CONTAIN MORE PLASTIC THAN FISH (BY WEIGHT).

World Economic Forum

☐ Today I picked up plastic and other trash and put it in a recycling bin.

FILTHY WATER CANNOT BE WASHED.

West African proverb

☐ Today I lobbied my congressional representatives to enforce the Save Our Seas Act.

DATE: __/__/__

HOW LONG WILL THIS TRASH BE AROUND?

paper	2–4 weeks
plastic-coated paper	5 years
plastic bags	10–20 years
plastic bottles	indefinitely
plastic six-pack holders	100 years
orange/banana peels	up to 2 years
aluminum cans	80–100 years
styrofoam	indefinitely
tin cans	50 years
nylon fabric	30–40 years
cotton shirt	1–6 months
glass bottles	1,000,000 years
wool socks	1–5 years

National Park Service

☐ Today, after reading this list, I decided to:

_____

_____

_____

Don't judge each day by the harvest you reap but by the seeds that you plant.

Robert Louis Stevenson, attributed

☐ Today I planted a seed of environmentalism by posting the list from the opposite page on social media.

DATE: __/__/__

- Worldwide obesity has nearly tripled since 1975.
- Obesity and being overweight kill more people than being underweight.
- Being overweight increases the risk of health problems, including heart disease and stroke, diabetes, osteoarthritis, and certain cancers.
- Obesity is preventable.

World Health Organization

Today I will: ☐ join or set up a CSA (Community Supported Agriculture) program in my neighborhood so that we have a regular source of fresh, locally grown food

☐ join or set up a regular running, walking, biking, sports, or exercise program in my neighborhood

DATE: __/__/__

WE MAY FIND IN THE LONG RUN THAT TINNED FOOD IS A DEADLIER WEAPON THAN THE MACHINE GUN.

George Orwell

Today I will lobby this _____ to:
food manufacturer

- ☐ reduce the fat, sugar, and salt in its processed foods
- ☐ restrict marketing of foods high in fats, sugars, and salt—especially those aimed at children and teenagers
- ☐ offer more nutritious products

DATE: __ / __ / __

TODAY I SAID THAT I WOULD DO THIS:

_____

_____

_____

_____

_____

_____

DATE: __ / __ / __

THIS IS WHAT I DID TODAY:

_____

_____

_____

_____

_____

_____

Saying
is one thing
and doing
is another.

Michel de Montaigne

DATE: __ / __ / __

No one would remember the Good Samaritan if he'd only had good intentions. He had money as well.

Margaret Thatcher

Today I made a big contribution to_____ because:

_____

_____

_____

_____

_____

_____

DATE: __/__/__

Give all thou can'st, high Heaven rejects the lore Of nicely calculated less or more.

William Wordsworth

Today I made a big contribution to_____ because:

_____

_____

_____

_____

_____

_____

DATE: __ / __ / __

HELPING HAND

Like more than
15 percent of people
in the world, Tish Hevel's father
suffered from a brain disease. When he died in 2015,
his family discovered that while there is a critical need for both
diseased and healthy postmortem brains for research, brains are not
generally included in organ donation programs. Hevel created the
nonprofit Brain Donor Project (braindonorproject.org) to raise awareness
and to make donating easier.

Tish Hevel's story inspired me to:

_____

_____

_____

_____

_____

_____

DATE: __ / __ / __

I AM THRILLED THAT THIS IS THE
IMPACT, ONE OF THE IMPACTS,
THAT MY FATHER HAS HAD
AND CONTINUES TO HAVE ON
CONTRIBUTING TO THE WORLD.

Tish Hevel

☐ Today I arranged for any organ donations that I want to be made
after my death.

Green, how I love you, green. Green wind. Green branches.

Federico García Lorca

Something new I did to go greener today:

_____

_____

_____

_____

_____

_____

_____

DATE: __/__/__

"GOOD" TO GO.

☐ Today I packed a daily go bag to eliminate the need for single-use plastic.

CHECKLIST:
☐ cloth bag
☐ glass food-storage container
☐ travel mug
☐ water bottle
☐ bamboo or metal cutlery
☐ paper straw
☐ cloth napkin to use as a plate

DATE: __ / __ / __

WHAT I TRIED TO DO TO HELP BUT FAILED TODAY:

_____

_____

_____

_____

_____

_____

_____

DATE: __ / __ / __

HOW I AGAIN TRIED TO HELP TODAY AFTER A FAILURE:

_____

_____

_____

_____

_____

_____

We try often, though we fall back often.

Walt Whitman

DATE: __ / __ / __

Peace is not an accident. Peace is not a gift. Peace is something we must all work for, every day, in every country.

Ban Ki-moon

How I worked for peace in the world today:

_____

_____

_____

_____

_____

_____

_____

DATE: __ / __ / __

An estimated **535** million children—nearly one in four—live in countries affected by conflict or disaster, often without access to medical care, quality education, proper nutrition, and protection.

UNICEF

☐ Today I marked International Day of Peace (September 21) on my calendar as a day for action.

DATE: __ / __ / __

ANIMAL WATCH

GIANT IBIS

The giant ibis, which is found mainly in northern Cambodia, has been designated as the most endangered bird in the world. Only 100 breeding pairs are believed to still live in the wild. This unique species is the victim of shrinking habitat, droughts, and hunters.

Today I: ☐ learned more about the plight of the giant ibis

☐ joined a bird conservation group

DATE: __/__/__

Everyone likes birds. What wild creature is more accessible to our eyes and ears?

David Attenborough

☐ Today I marked National Audubon Day (April 26) on my calendar as a day of action for all birds.

DATE: __ / __ / __

Livestock production contributes more to climate change than all of the world's cars, trucks, buses, trains, planes, ships, and rocket ships combined.

United Nations

Today I will: ☐ reduce my consumption of meat by following VB6 (Vegan Before 6:00 p.m.)

☐ create a diet plan of my own with less meat than I am eating now

THE ONLY MENACE IS INERTIA.

Saint-John Perse

☐ Today I will encourage others to change their eating habits now!

We become just by
performing just
actions, temperate
by performing
temperate actions,
brave by performing
brave actions.

Aristotle

DATE: __ / __ / __

A JUST ACTION I PERFORMED TODAY:

_____

_____

_____

_____

_____

_____

DATE: __ / __ / __

A BRAVE ACTION I PERFORMED TODAY:

_____

_____

_____

_____

_____

_____

THE ARTS ARE . . . ONE OF THE
THINGS THAT MAKE THIS COUNTRY
STRONG. WE ALWAYS THINK IT'S
OUR ECONOMY OR OUR MILITARY
POWER, BUT IN FACT, I THINK IT'S
OUR CULTURE, OUR CIVILIZATION,
OUR IDEAS, OUR CREATIVITY.

Caroline Kennedy

Our country's cultural contribution to the world that makes me most
proud:

_____

_____

_____

_____

_____

ART WILL MAKE OUR STREETS AS BEAUTIFUL AS THE WOODS, AS ELEVATING AS THE MOUNTAIN-SIDES.

William Morris

☐ Today I noticed this uplifting work of public art:

_____

_____

_____

_____

_____

DATE: __/__/__

Community Service Day

**Do one of these important
services today. Check the box.**

☐ Read to a blind person.

☐ Walk a shelter dog.

☐ Shop for an elderly neighbor.

☐ Collect toys/toiletries for a

homeless shelter.

☐ Donate used clothes or furniture.

☐ Support veterans or military

families.

☐ Be an English-conversation

partner.

☐ Donate blood.

☐ Prepare taxes as a volunteer.

☐ Teach healthy cooking.

☐ Deliver meals to shut-ins.

☐ Welcome a new neighbor.

☐ Thank a firefighter, police officer,

or veteran.

☐ _____

something else

DATE: __ / __ / __

Those who are happiest are those who do the most for others.

Booker T. Washington

What I did for someone else today:

_____

_____

_____

_____

_____

_____

_____

_____

About 40 percent of US rivers and lakes are too polluted for fishing.

Natural Resources Defense Council

☐ Today I will lobby my congressional representatives to push for enforcement of the Clean Water Act.

EVERYONE LIVES DOWNSTREAM FROM SOMEONE ELSE.

American proverb

☐ Today I will check the level of lead and other pollutants in my community's water.

[Morning question]
What good shall I do this day?

[Evening question]
What good have I done today?

Benjamin Franklin

DATE: __ / __ / __

[MORNING QUESTION] WHAT GOOD SHALL I DO THIS DAY?

_____

_____

_____

_____

_____

_____

DATE: __ / __ / __

[EVENING QUESTION] WHAT GOOD HAVE I DONE TODAY?

_____

_____

_____

_____

_____

HOW CAN YOU
WORSHIP A
HOMELESS MAN
ON SUNDAY
AND IGNORE
ONE ON
MONDAY?

Coalition for the Homeless

DATE: __ / __ / __

☐ TODAY I WILL COLLECT SCHOOL SUPPLIES FOR CHILDREN LIVING
    IN A SHELTER.

DATE: __ / __ / __

☐ TODAY I WILL COLLECT WINTER COATS FOR PEOPLE LIVING
    IN A SHELTER.

DATE: __ / __ / __

VOLUNTEERISM

Where I volunteer:

_____

_____

_____

Where I would like to volunteer:

_____

_____

_____

How often I volunteer: __ hours per

☐ week

☐ month

How often I would like

to volunteer: __ hours per

☐ week

☐ month

Rate yourself as a volunteer (from 1 to 10, with

10 being the greatest): _____

DATE: __ / __ / __

And so, my fellow Americans, ask not what your country can do for you—ask what you can do for your country.

John F. Kennedy

What I can do for my country:

_____

_____

_____

_____

_____

_____

_____

DATE: __ / __ / __

One billion people, or 15 percent
of the world's population,
experience some form of disability,
and disability prevalence is higher
for developing countries.

The World Bank

**To help people with disabilities be fully included in the economic and
social life of our community, today I will work for:**

☐ accessible physical environments and transportation

☐ availability of assistive devices and technologies

☐ adapted means of communication

☐ uninterrupted service delivery

☐ elimination of stigma and prejudice

DATE: __ / __ / __

What I learned was that these athletes were not disabled, they were super-abled. The Olympics is where heroes are made. The Paralympics is where heroes come.

Joey Reiman

A super-abled athlete I admire today:

_____

_____

_____

_____

_____

DATE: __ / __ / __

I UNREASONABLY INSIST ON THIS CHANGE IN MY COMMUNITY:

_____

_____

_____

_____

_____

_____

DATE: __ / __ / __

I UNREASONABLY INSIST ON THIS CHANGE IN MY COUNTRY:

_____

_____

_____

_____

_____

_____

The reasonable man adapts himself to the world: the unreasonable one persists in trying to adapt the world to himself. Therefore all progress depends on the unreasonable man.

George Bernard Shaw

DATE: __/__/__

The best time to plant a tree was 20 years ago. The second best time is now.

Chinese proverb

A belated action I took today to help the environment:

_____

_____

_____

_____

_____

_____

_____

DATE: __/__/__

IT IS NEVER TOO LATE TO DO RIGHT.

Ralph Waldo Emerson

A belated action I took today to help create a more just society:

_____

_____

_____

_____

_____

_____

_____

DATE: __/__/__

HELPING HAND

On Sundays, after
a week of working as
a professional hairstylist at
an expensive New York salon, Mark Bustos offers free
haircuts to homeless people on the streets and in the parks.
"We all know what it feels like to get a good haircut," he has said.
He was inspired by a visit to family in the Philippines, where he decided
to help the many poor children he saw by styling their hair for free.
In 2014, he started the charity #BeAwesomeToSomebody.

Mark Bustos's story inspired me to:

_____

_____

_____

_____

_____

_____

PEOPLE ASK ME IF I CAN COME OUT WITH YOU OR JOIN YOUR TEAM. MY ANSWER IS JUST GO AND DO IT.

Mark Bustos

☐ Today I just went and shared _____ with someone
                                       my talent
who needed it.

DATE: __ / __ / __

Upcycling is also known as creative reuse, a different process from recycling but with the same goal—to reduce waste. Upcycling transforms an unwanted item into something new and desirable.

Draw something you upcycled today:

The purpose—where I start—is the idea of use. It is not recycling. It's reuse.

Issey Miyake

Draw a piece of clothing that you creatively reused today:

I BELIEVE THAT EVERY RIGHT IMPLIES A RESPONSIBILITY; EVERY OPPORTUNITY, AN OBLIGATION; EVERY POSSESSION, A DUTY.

John D. Rockefeller

DATE: __ / __ / __

MY RIGHT TO _____ GIVES ME THIS RESPONSIBILITY:

_____

_____

_____

DATE: __ / __ / __

MY OPPORTUNITY FOR _____ GIVES ME THIS OBLIGATION:

_____

_____

_____

DATE: __ / __ / __

MY POSSESSION OF _____ GIVES ME THIS DUTY:

_____

_____

_____

DATE: __/__/__

One of the biggest challenges we have
to our democracy is the degree to
which we don't share a common
baseline of facts. . . . At a certain
point, you just live in a bubble.
And that's part of why our politics
is so polarized right now.

Barack Obama

☐ Today I read outside my political bubble and learned this, which is
worth considering:

_____

_____

_____

_____

_____

_____

ALTERNATIVE FACTS
ARE NOT FACTS.
THEY'RE FALSEHOODS.

Chuck Todd

☐ Today I double-checked this "fact" I heard or read on the Internet
before repeating it:

_____

_____

_____

_____

_____

It was a ☐ fact ☐ falsehood.

DATE: __ / __ / __

ANIMAL WATCH

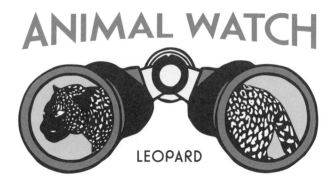

LEOPARD

The Amur leopard is the world's rarest wildcat. A recent study counted only 84 in China and Russia. The animal is poached mostly for its spotted fur, but the scarcity of prey has also contributed to its decline. The Russian government established a new protected area, Land of the Leopard National Park, in 2012.

Today I: ☐ read more about leopards

☐ marked International Leopard Day (May 3) on my calendar as a day for action

I THINK SOMETIMES WE NEED TO TAKE A STEP BACK AND JUST REMEMBER WE HAVE NO GREATER RIGHT TO BE HERE THAN ANY OTHER ANIMAL.

David Attenborough

☐ Today I attended a meeting of a wildlife conservation organization.

If allowed to survive, this grass will produce enough oxygen for two students to breathe for one semester.

▲
▼

Lawn sign, University of Iowa

☐ Today I volunteered to work in a nature preserve or a public park.

I believe a leaf of grass is no less than the journey-work of the stars.

Walt Whitman

☐ Today I took a walk and appreciated the nature around me.

DATE: __ / __ / __

THE GREATEST CRISIS I SEE TODAY:

_____

_____

_____

_____

_____

_____

_____

DATE: __ / __ / __

THE OPPORTUNITY A CRISIS GIVES ME FOR ACTION TODAY:

_____

_____

_____

_____

_____

_____

In the Chinese language, the word "crisis" is composed of two characters, one representing danger and the other, opportunity.

危机

John F. Kennedy

Because democracy demands wisdom, **NEH** serves and strengthens our republic by promoting excellence in the humanities and conveying the lessons of history to all Americans.

National Endowment for the Humanities

Today I think democracy demands this specific wisdom:

_____

_____

_____

_____

_____

_____

DATE: __/__/__

Those who cannot remember the past are condemned to repeat it.

George Santayana

A lesson from history that motivates my political activism today:

_____

_____

_____

_____

_____

DATE: __/__/__

DONATION DAY

INTERNATIONAL RELIEF AND DEVELOPMENT

Today I researched these organizations through a nonprofit charity watch-dog organization, such as **Charity Navigator**, **CharityWatch**, or **GuideStar**.

☐ CARE

☐ International Rescue Committee

☐ Partners In Health

☐ Rotary International

☐ United Methodist Committee on Relief

☐ _____

another organization

DATE: __ / __ / __

Give to another human being without the expectation of a return.

Bill Bradley

Today I gave $_____ / _____
                                              goods/services
to this international relief and development organization:

_____

_____

because:

_____

_____

_____

WHERE HAVE ALL THE FLOWERS GONE?

Pete Seeger

☐ Today I planted flowers in a window box or in my garden for the pleasure of all.

As we manure the flowerbeds, for the plants, so they manure the air beds for us.

Novalis

☐ Today I planted in a community garden.

DATE: __ / __ / __

A STRONG BELIEF I HOLD ABOUT JUSTICE:

_____

_____

_____

_____

_____

_____

DATE: __ / __ / __

WHAT I DID TODAY THAT REFLECTS MY BELIEF ABOUT JUSTICE:

_____

_____

_____

_____

_____

We know what
a person thinks
not when he
tells us what
he thinks, but
by his actions.

Isaac Bashevis Singer

DATE: __ / __ / __

The United States spends **16.2 percent**
of its GDP on social programs; similarly
developed countries spend **21.3 percent.**
Social programs like veterans' benefits
and unemployment compensation can
make a huge difference in a country's
poverty rate.

The Borgen Project

☐ Today I lobbied my congressional representatives to spend more
money on social programs.

DATE: __ / __ / __

THE ULTIMATE MORAL TEST OF ANY GOVERNMENT IS THE WAY IT TREATS THREE GROUPS OF ITS CITIZENS. FIRST, THOSE IN THE DAWN OF LIFE—OUR CHILDREN. SECOND, THOSE IN THE SHADOWS OF LIFE—OUR NEEDY, OUR SICK, OUR HANDICAPPED. THIRD, THOSE IN THE TWILIGHT OF LIFE—OUR ELDERLY.

Hubert Humphrey

Rate the United States (from 1 to 5, with 5 being the greatest) on the way you think it treats:

children: _____

the elderly: _____

the sick: _____

the needy: _____

the handicapped: _____

DATE: __ / __ / __

Test Your Knowledge

THE CARBON FOOTPRINT OF FOOD CHOICES

Rank these foods in the order of their negative impact on the environment (from 1, the worst, to 8).

☐ wheat

☐ lamb

☐ fish

☐ nuts

☐ pork

☐ rice

☐ chicken

☐ beef

Answers: 8, 1, 5, 6, 3, 7, 4, 2

If the world's diet doesn't change, we simply can't avoid the worst effects of climate change.

Caroline Lucas

Today I will make this change in my diet to reduce my carbon footprint:

_____

_____

_____

_____

_____

_____

[The issue of childhood obesity.] is critically important to me because it's critically important to the health and success of our kids, and of this nation, ultimately.

Michelle Obama

DATE: __ / __ / __

☐ **TODAY I WILL ADVOCATE FOR HEALTHIER CHOICES IN SCHOOL CAFETERIAS.**

DATE: __ / __ / __

☐ **TODAY I WILL ADVOCATE FOR DAILY PHYSICAL ACTIVITY FOR CHILDREN AT SCHOOL.**

DATE: __ / __ / __

A LOCAL PROBLEM I SEE CLEARLY:

_____

_____

_____

_____

_____

_____

DATE: __ / __ / __

WHAT I DID TODAY TO HELP SOLVE A LOCAL PROBLEM:

_____

_____

_____

_____

_____

_____

To see a problem clearly is three parts of the way to solving it.

J. A. Hadfield

We have a single mission: to protect and hand on the planet to the next generation.

François Hollande

My greatest concern for the world of my children and grandchildren:

_____

_____

_____

_____

_____

_____

_____

DATE: __ / __ / __

I LIKE THE DREAMS OF THE FUTURE BETTER THAN THE HISTORY OF THE PAST.

Thomas Jefferson

My dream for the future:

_____

_____

_____

_____

_____

_____

HELPING HAND

As warden of Volcanoes National Park in Rwanda, Edwin Sabuhoro tried to protect the endangered mountain gorillas. When tracking down poachers was not effective enough, he turned poachers into farmers, using his own savings at first for land and seeds. The farming program has since grown into a nonprofit, the Iby'Iwacu Cultural Village (cbtrwanda.org), which helps generate income through tourism, giving local people an incentive to conserve the park.

Edwin Sabuhoro's story inspired me to:

_____

_____

_____

_____

_____

_____

WE CAN'T AFFORD TO FAIL THE WILDLIFE. IT WAS PASSED ON TO US BY ANCESTORS, AND WE HAVE TO WORK HARD TO MAKE SURE THAT WE PASS IT ON TO THE NEXT GENERATION.

Edwin Sabuhoro

☐ Today I will add an ecotourism vacation to a fragile area to the top of my bucket list to support conservation.

TODAY I COMMIT TO LOOK

☐  on recyclable materials. This universal symbol represents a three-step process: **reduce, reuse, recycle.**

☐  on fresh and processed foods. "Organic" indicates that the product has been produced through methods appoved by the US Department of Agriculture.

☐  on coffee, tea, chocolate, honey, nuts, and grains. Products with this label are made by a more equitable global trade model that benefits farmers, workers, consumers, industry, and the earth.

ING FOR THESE LABELS:

 on meat, poultry, dairy, eggs. The animals have been raised with compassion and respect and in an environment that supports their ability to engage in all their natural behaviors.

 on wood and forestry products. Products with this label come from responsibly managed forests.

 on cosmetics, personal care products, pet care products. No new animal testing is used in any phase of development of products with this label.

DATE: __ / __ / __

☐ Did it.

IT IS NOT ENOUGH TO DO GOOD; ONE MUST DO IT IN A GOOD WAY.

Marquis de Condorcet

DATE: __ / __ / __

GOOD I DID IN MY COMMUNITY TODAY:

_____

_____

_____

_____

_____

_____

DATE: __ / __ / __

THE GOOD WAY I HELPED MY COMMUNITY TODAY:

_____

_____

_____

_____

_____

DATE: __ / __ / __

Sample Political Letter

Dear [Senator/Representative] _____,

I am writing as your constituent in [state] and also as a patriotic American citizen. I am very concerned about a vote that is coming up soon in Congress [details of bill]. I believe that it is important that you vote [for/against] this bill because it will have [this impact] on [state] and [this impact] on our country. I look forward to discussing this at your next town hall.

Sincerely,

_____

☐ Today I wrote to [Senator/Representative] _____

   because _____

   _____

   _____

   _____

DATE: __ / __ / __

Congress shall make no law . . . prohibiting . . . the right of the people . . . to petition the Government for a redress of grievances.

First Amendment, US Constitution

HOW TO CONTACT CONGRESS

Senators:

https://www.senate.gov/general/contact_information/senators_cfm.cfm.

Representatives: https://www.house.gov/representatives. (Note: Some representatives accept e-mails only from constituents.)

☐ Today I wrote to [Senator/Representative] _____ about this

   issue: _____

☐ Today I organized a letter/e-mail-writing campaign to [Senator/

   Representative] _____ about this

   issue: _____

   _____

ANIMAL WATCH

PORPOISE

Two porpoises are considered "critically endangered." The Yangtze finless porpoise is threatened mainly by overfishing, which has diminished its food supply. Vaquita porpoises get entangled in nets meant to trawl for other fish. There may be as few as 30 vaquitas left in the world.

Today I:
☐ read more about international fishing laws
☐ marked International Save the Vaquita Day
(first Saturday after July 4) on my calendar
as a day for action

who hears the fishes when they cry?

Henry David Thoreau

☐ Today I explored the American Cetacean Society website (acsonline.org) to learn more about saving the vaquita.

DATE: __/__/__

What's Wrong with Bottled Water, Anyway?

- Thirty-six ounces of water is needed to produce one 12-ounce plastic water bottle.
- Fifty percent of bottled water is repackaged tap water.
- Bottling water produces 2.5 million tons of carbon dioxide yearly.
- One billion dollars' worth of plastic is dumped in US landfills every year.
- Seventeen million barrels of oil are consumed in yearly production of water bottles, enough to run 1 million cars for a year.
- Americans spend more than $11 billion a year on bottled water.
- Fifteen hundred water bottles are consumed in the United States every second.
- One billion water bottles are shipped across the United States weekly.
- Tap water is cheap, safe, eco-friendly.

▲
Department of Utilities, Leesburg, Virginia
▼

☐ Okay, I get it already.

THE FREE MARKET SHOULD NOT INCLUDE THE RIGHT TO POLLUTE OUR ENVIRONMENT.

George McGovern

☐ From today on I will give up wasteful bottled water and use a thermos.

DATE: __ / __ / __

PEOPLE WHO CALL OUT THE BEST IN ME:

_____

_____

_____

_____

_____

_____

DATE: __ / __ / __

☐ **TODAY** _____ **INSPIRED ME TO DO THIS GOOD:**

_____

_____

_____

_____

_____

_____

The people
I admire are the
people that lead
by calling out
the best of who
we are.

Cory Booker

DATE: __ / __ / __

In the 21st century, libraries of all types are responding to the changing social, economic, and political impacts of living in a digital society.

American Library Association

At the library today I:
- ☐ took a computer class
- ☐ searched for a job
- ☐ attended a lecture or a class
- ☐ attended an adult literacy class
- ☐ used assistive technology
- ☐ learned how to download e-books and films online
- ☐ borrowed a printed book
- ☐ _____

  other

WITHOUT LIBRARIES WHAT HAVE WE? WE HAVE NO PAST AND NO FUTURE.

Ray Bradbury

☐ Today I will ask my local library how I can help.

DATE: __/__/__

Community Service Day

**Do one of these important
services today. Check the box.**

☐ Read to a blind person.

☐ Walk a shelter dog.

☐ Shop for an elderly neighbor.

☐ Collect toys/toiletries for a
homeless shelter.

☐ Donate used clothes or furniture.

☐ Support veterans or military
families.

☐ Be an English-conversation
partner.

☐ Donate blood.

☐ Prepare taxes as a volunteer.

☐ Teach healthy cooking.

☐ Deliver meals to shut-ins.

☐ Welcome a new neighbor.

☐ Thank a firefighter, police officer,
or veteran.

☐ _____
something else

Shall we make a new rule of life from tonight: always to try to be a little kinder than necessary?

J. M. Barrie

How I was a little kinder today:

_____

_____

_____

_____

_____

_____

_____

DATE: __/__/__

Open your eyes to whether your city is truly accessible for everyone—every curb cut or lack thereof—for the disabled, people of all ages, and for every parent with a stroller. Find ways to travel a mile in their shoes or chairs, and listen to them. Then amplify their voices in calling for improvements.

Brent Toderian

☐ Today I advocated for this change to make my neighborhood more accessible:

_____

_____

_____

_____

_____

What does this international symbol for the disabled indicate?

Check the correct answer(s).

☐ The vehicle is driven by a disabled person.

☐ The parking spot is reserved for a disabled person.

☐ The lavatory can accommodate a wheelchair user.

☐ A button can activate the door.

☐ The transit station or vehicle is accessible.

☐ The transit route uses accessible vehicles.

Answer: All of the above

TOMORROW IS NOW.

Eleanor Roosevelt

DATE: __ / __ / __

TODAY **I SPOKE OUT ABOUT:**

_____

_____

_____

_____

_____

_____

DATE: __ / __ / __

TODAY **I TOOK THIS ACTION:**

_____

_____

_____

_____

_____

DATE: __ / __ / __

In 2017, 68.5 million people worldwide were forcibly displaced from their homes because of persecution, conflict, violence, or human rights violations. This number is larger than the entire population of the United Kingdom.

▲

United Nations High Commissioner for Refugees, Global Trends Study

▼

☐ Today I will support or volunteer at an organization that helps displaced people.

When I came here as a child, I will never forget sailing into New York Harbor for the first time and beholding the Statue of Liberty. I did not have to face refugee camps or the kind of danger that many refugees endure. But like all refugees, I shared a hope to live a safe life with dignity and a chance to give back to my new country.

Madeleine Albright

☐ Today I shared the story of a refugee who gave back to our country.

PHILANTHROPY

Charities I support:

_____

_____

_____

Other charities I would like to support:

_____

_____

_____

How much money/goods I donated last year:

_____

_____

How much money/goods I hope to donate this
year:

_____

_____

Rate yourself as a philanthropist (from 1 to 10, with
10 being the greatest): _____

DATE: __ / __ / __

Everyone knows about Black Friday and Cyber Monday. Now help me spread the word about Giving Tuesday.

Bill Gates

Today I: ☐ marked Giving Tuesday (the Tuesday following Thanksgiving) on my calendar with a note to make a charitable donation

☐ spread the word about Giving Tuesday to others

DATE: __ /__ /__

TELL ME WHAT YOU EAT, AND I WILL TELL YOU WHAT YOU ARE.

Jean Anthelme Brillat-Savarin

This is what I ate today:

_____

_____

_____

_____

So I am a:

_____

_____

DATE: __ / __ / __

THE FREEZER IS THE FOOD-WASTE WARRIOR'S BEST FRIEND.

Dana Gunders

Today I: ☐ checked the website of the US Department of Agriculture (www.fsis.usda.gov) for tips on freezing

☐ had my weekly "freezer night" meal

The vehemence
of the current
dialogue fills me
with hope. . . .
It's only when we
do care that we
have the possibility
of something better.

Sonia Sotomayor

DATE: __/__/__

I CARE VEHEMENTLY ABOUT THIS COMMUNITY ISSUE:

_____

_____

_____

_____

_____

_____

DATE: __/__/__

I CARE VEHEMENTLY ABOUT THIS WORLD ISSUE:

_____

_____

_____

_____

_____

To become a true global citizen, one must abandon all notions of "otherness."

Suzy Kassem

How I contributed to interfaith understanding today:

_____

_____

_____

_____

_____

_____

_____

A civilization is to be judged by its treatment of minorities.

Mahatma Gandhi

How I contributed to racial understanding today:

_____

_____

_____

_____

_____

_____

HELPING HAND

In 2012, Luke Mickelson of Twin Falls, Idaho, discovered that some kids in his community were sleeping on piles of clothes because their parents couldn't afford to buy them beds. He built 11 bunk beds in his garage that year, and by 2018 the charity he started had built and delivered more than 1,500 beds. Sleep in Heavenly Peace (shpbeds.org) provides construction manuals and training courses for the volunteers in its 152 chapters in 41 states.

Luke Mickelson's story inspired me to:

_____

_____

_____

_____

_____

_____

DATE: __ / __ / __

NO KID SLEEPS
ON THE FLOOR
IN OUR TOWN.

Sleep in Heavenly Peace motto

My motto: No Kid _____

      in Our Town.

DATE: __/__/__

The planet has a fever. If your baby has a fever . . . [and] the doctor says you need to intervene here, you don't say, "Well, I read a science-fiction novel that tells me it's not a problem."

Al Gore

☐ Today I educated myself on the scientific facts of climate change so that I can educate others in public and private discussions.

DATE: __ / __ / __

The planet's average surface temperature has risen about 1.62 degrees Fahrenheit since the late 19th century, a change driven largely by increased carbon dioxide and other human-made emissions into the atmosphere. Most of the warming occurred in the past 35 years, with the five warmest years on record taking place since 2010.

NASA

☐ Today I demanded that my local and federal government representatives work to combat climate change by supporting national measures and joining worldwide coalitions.

DATE: __ / __ / __

HOW I WAS A PEACEMAKER TODAY:

_____

_____

_____

_____

_____

_____

DATE: __ / __ / __

HOW I WAS A HEALER TODAY:

_____

_____

_____

_____

_____

_____

The planet does not need more successful people. But it does desperately need more peacemakers, healers, restorers, storytellers, and lovers of every kind.

David W. Orr

THE ROOTS OF TOBACCO PLANTS MUST GO CLEAR THROUGH TO HELL.

Thomas Alva Edison

☐ Today I will publicize these benefits of quitting smoking, according
to the Centers for Disease Control and Prevention:

- After 1 year, the increased risk of a heart attack drops sharply.
- Within 2 to 5 years, the increased risk of a stroke may be
  about that of a nonsmoker's.
- Within 5 years, increased risks of mouth, throat, esophagus,
  and bladder cancer drop by half.
- After 10 years, the increased risk of dying from lung cancer
  drops by half.

DATE: ___ / ___ / ___

In 2018, 27 percent of high school students said they used tobacco for one or more days in a month. Among all tobacco products, including cigarettes, chewing tobacco, and hookah, e-cigarettes—also known as vapes— were the ones most commonly used by teens.

Centers for Disease Control and Prevention

Today I: ☐ talked to _____ about the dangers of any kind
a teenager
of smoking, including e-cigarettes

☐ joined the campaign to raise the legal smoking age

ANIMAL WATCH

ORANGUTAN

The orangutan shares 96.4 percent of our genes. As the largest mammal that lives in trees, it is vital to seed dispersal. Endangered because of its extremely low reproduction rates, the orangutan is also being decimated by poaching, deforestation, and the pet trade.

Today I: ☐ read more about the orangutan

☐ marked International Orangutan Day (August 19) on my calendar as a day for action

Chimpanzees, gorillas, orangutans have been living for hundreds of thousands of years in their forest. . . . I would say that they have been in a way more successful than us as far as being in harmony with the environment.

Jane Goodall

☐ Today I told others on social media about the plight of the orangutan and the dangers of deforestation.

More skin cancers are diagnosed in the United States each year than all other cancers combined. Exposure to ultraviolet rays is the primary cause, mostly from the sun, but also from indoor tanning beds and sunlamps. To protect yourself and others, use this catchphrase:

Slip! Slop! Slap!® and Wrap

- Slip on a shirt.
- Slop on sunscreen.
- Slap on a hat.
- Wrap on sunglasses to protect the eyes and skin around them.

American Cancer Society

DATE: __ / __ / __

☐ TODAY I MEMORIZED SLIP! SLOP! SLAP!® AND WRAP.

DATE: __ / __ / __

☐ TODAY I TAUGHT THIS CATCHPHRASE TO OTHERS.

NO MATTER WHAT PEOPLE TELL YOU, WORDS AND IDEAS CAN CHANGE THE WORLD.

Robin Williams

This is a word or an idea that changed my worldview:

_____

_____

_____

_____

_____

_____

_____

DATE: __ / __ / __

It is time for parents to teach young people early on that in diversity there is beauty and there is strength.

Maya Angelou

☐ Today I shared this vision of diversity with a young person:

_____

_____

_____

_____

_____

_____

_____

DATE: __ /__ /__

MY VISION FOR EDUCATION IS:

_____

_____

_____

_____

_____

_____

DATE: __ /__ /__

ACTION I TOOK TODAY TO CARRY OUT MY EDUCATIONAL VISION:

_____

_____

_____

_____

_____

_____

VISION WITHOUT
ACTION IS MERELY
A DREAM. ACTION
WITHOUT VISION
JUST PASSES THE TIME.
VISION WITH ACTION
CAN CHANGE THE
WORLD.

Joel Arthur Barker

DATE: __ / __ / __

DONATION DAY

— LITERACY

Today I researched these organizations through a nonprofit charity watch-dog organization, such as **Charity Navigator**, **CharityWatch**, or **GuideStar**.

- [ ] Barbara Bush Foundation for Family Literacy
- [ ] Literacy Action
- [ ] The Literacy Lab
- [ ] Literacy Partners Inc.
- [ ] Reach Out and Read
- [ ] _____
  another organization

Literacy is . . . the road to human progress and the means through which every man, woman, and child can realize his or her full potential.

Kofi Annan

Today I gave $_____ / _____
goods/services
to this literacy organization:

_____

_____

because:

_____

_____

_____

DATE: __ / __ / __

In 2016, the level of carbon dioxide emissions from transportation surpassed the emissions from the power sector—a trend that is projected to continue through at least 2040.

▲
US Energy Information Administration
▼

☐ Today I researched electric, hybrid, and flex-fuel cars for purchase or rental.

Environmental pollution is an incurable disease. It can only be prevented.

Barry Commoner

Today I helped to prevent pollution from transportation by:

- ☐ enrolling in a car-share program
- ☐ joining a car pool or using public transportation to get to work and back

Each morning sees
some task begin,
Each evening sees it
close;
Something attempted,
something done,
Has earned a night's
repose.

Henry Wadsworth Longfellow

DATE: __ / __ / __

HOW I EARNED A NIGHT'S REPOSE BY HELPING THE NEEDY TODAY:

_____

_____

_____

_____

_____

_____

DATE: __ / __ / __

HOW I EARNED A NIGHT'S REPOSE BY HELPING THE ENVIRONMENT TODAY:

_____

_____

_____

_____

_____

_____

In 2016, 152 million 5- to 17-year-olds were in child labor. Forty-eight percent of them were 5 to 11 years old.

International Labour Organization

☐ Today I learned more about child labor and shared the information with others.

DATE: ___ / ___ / ___

Child labor perpetuates poverty. . . . If the children are deprived [of] education, then they are bound to remain poor.

Kailash Satyarthi

☐ Today I marked World Day Against Child Labour (June 12) on my calendar as a day for action.

Test Your Knowledge

AIR POLLUTION

_____

_____

1) How many deaths does air pollution cause worldwide?

a) 1 in 8   b) 1 in 20   c) 1 in 100   d) 1 in 200

2) What percentage of the global population lives in places with unhealthy air quality?

a) 50 percent   b) 75 percent   c) 20 percent   d) 92 percent in 200

3) Of these countries, which one has the worst pollution?

a) Mexico   b) United States   c) China   d) France

4) Of these countries, which one has the cleanest air?

a) United States   b) Finland   c) Great Britain   d) Brazil

Answers: a, d, c, b

Air pollution is turning Mother Nature prematurely gray.

Irv Kupcinet

How I helped to preserve Mother Nature today:

_____

_____

_____

_____

_____

_____

_____

_____

Nearly one in five adults in the United States lives with a mental illness (46.6 million in 2017).

National Institute of Mental Health

☐ Today I encouraged and helped someone who was suffering emotionally to find professional help.

EVERYONE MUST KEEP UP THE
STRUGGLE [AGAINST DEPRESSION],
FOR IT IS ALWAYS LIKELY THAT
YOU WILL WIN THE BATTLE AND
NEARLY A CERTAINTY YOU WILL
WIN THE WAR.

William Styron

☐ Today I will volunteer at, support, or help to publicize a mental health
hotline.

DATE: __ / __ / __

A CAUSE THAT MOVED ME TODAY:

_____

_____

_____

_____

_____

_____

DATE: __ / __ / __

A CAUSE THAT EMBOLDENED ME TODAY:

_____

_____

_____

_____

_____

_____

A good
cause
makes a
stout heart
and a
strong arm.

▲
Proverb
▼

DATE: __/__/__

I had promised myself when I was 13 or 14 that if I ever made it, I was going to come back to communities like the South Bronx and try to help children have a chance. . . . Most of my friends never had a chance.

Geoffrey Canada

How I helped a child have a chance today:

_____

_____

_____

_____

_____

_____

_____

DATE: __ / __ / __

ANTICIPATE CHARITY BY PREVENTING POVERTY.

Moses Maimonides

How I advocated for just national policies on poverty today:

_____

_____

_____

_____

_____

_____

_____

HELPING HAND

In 2004, Luma Mufleh started a soccer program for refugee children in Clarkston, Georgia. Since then, Mufleh, a refugee from Jordan, has provided community support through her nonprofit, Fugees Family (fugeesfamily.org). After-school soccer and tutoring have grown into a year-round school tailored to these students, grades 6 to 12, who have experienced war and have gaps in language and education. The first graduates have all enrolled in college, and a new school opened in Ohio.

Luma Mufleh's story inspired me to:

_____

_____

_____

_____

_____

_____

DATE: __ /__ /__

When you've left your home, your family and everything you know to start new, that is very difficult. You don't have the education, the language, and you don't have someone that can broker things for you.

Luma Mufleh

Today I:　　☐ volunteered with children at a refugee center

　　　　　　☐ collected sports equipment for a refugee center

WINE HATH DROWNED MORE MEN THAN THE SEA.

Proverb

☐ Today I will drink responsibly.

☐ Today I will refrain from drinking and be a designated driver.

DATE: __ / __ / __

An estimated 88,000 people in the United States died from alcohol-related causes each year between 2006 and 2010. Alcohol abuse was the third leading preventable cause of death after (1) tobacco use and (2) poor diet and physical inactivity.

Centers for Disease Control
and Prevention

☐ Today I pledge not to drink excessively, as defined by the CDC, and
to intervene when others do:
- binge drinking: on a single occasion, 4 or more drinks for
a woman; 5 or more for a man
- heavy drinking: in a week, 8 or more drinks for a woman;
15 or more for a man

Hope begins in the dark, the stubborn hope that if you just show up and try to do the right thing, the dawn will come. You wait and watch and work: you don't give up.

Anne Lamott

DATE: ___/___/___

WHAT I WATCHED AND WAITED FOR TODAY:

_____

_____

_____

_____

_____

_____

DATE: ___/___/___

WHAT I WORKED ON TODAY:

_____

_____

_____

_____

_____

_____

DATE: __ / __ / __

Using a few carefully placed letters [to the editor], you can generate plenty of community discussion. You can also keep an issue going by preventing it from disappearing from the public eye.

Community Tool Box,
University of Kansas

How to Write a Letter to the Editor (adapted from Community Tool Box):

- Check online for specific submissions guidelines.
- Grab attention with your opening sentence.
- Explain quickly and concisely what the letter is about.
- Use plain language to explain why the issue is important.
- Give evidence and specific suggestions for what can be done.
- Be brief.

☐ Today I sent a letter to _____

about _____.

DATE: __/__/__

Words are capable of shaking the entire structure of government . . . words can prove mightier than ten military divisions.

Václav Havel

Today I expressed my opinion about _____

☐ on a radio talk show

☐ at a town meeting

☐ at a rally

☐ _____
          somewhere else

ANIMAL WATCH

TIGER

Tigers have lost 93 percent of their habitat to human encroachment. They are also killed by poachers, who sell every body part, including whiskers, as unproven medicines or status symbols. Yet, because of conservation efforts, the population of tigers in the wild has begun to grow after 100 years of decline. In 2010, the 13 Asian countries where tigers live set a goal of doubling their number to 6,000 by 2022, the Chinese Year of the Tiger.

Today I: ☐ read more about tigers

☐ marked Global Tiger Day (July 29) on my calendar as a day for action

DATE: __/__/__

Tigers are some of the most vital and beloved animals on Earth. . . . I am optimistic about what can be achieved when governments, communities, conservationists, and private foundations like ours come together to tackle global challenges.

Leonardo DiCaprio

Today I: ☐ joined a wildlife conservation organization

☐ educated others about the plight of the tiger

DATE: __/__/__

SEAT BELT USE IS ONE OF THE MOST EFFECTIVE WAYS TO SAVE LIVES AND REDUCE INJURIES IN MOTOR VEHICLE CRASHES. MORE THAN HALF OF THE PEOPLE WHO DIED IN CAR CRASHES IN 2016 WERE NOT BUCKLED UP AT THE TIME. REAR-SEAT PASSENGERS ARE LESS LIKELY TO WEAR A SEAT BELT, MAKING THEM MORE SUSCEPTIBLE TO INJURE THEMSELVES OR OTHER PASSENGERS.

▲
**Centers for Disease Control
and Prevention**
▼

Today I will: ☐ require everyone in my car to wear a seat belt

☐ wear a seat belt myself when I am in someone else's car

☐ advocate for a seat belt law that covers everyone, not just

those in the front seat

DATE: __ / __ / __

A TREE NEVER HITS AN AUTOMOBILE EXCEPT IN SELF-DEFENSE.

American proverb

From today on I will:
- [ ] drive within the speed limit
- [ ] obey all signs
- [ ] not text while driving

Within us all
there are wells
of thought
and dynamos
of energy
which are not
suspected until
emergencies
arrive.

Thomas J. Watson

DATE: __ / __ / __

AN EMERGENCY FOR ☐ THE WORLD ☐ THE COUNTRY ☐ THE COMMUNITY:

_____

_____

_____

DATE: __ / __ / __

MY IDEA FOR DEALING WITH IT TODAY:

_____

_____

_____

DATE: __ / __ / __

MY ACTION FOR DEALING WITH IT TODAY:

_____

_____

_____

DATE: __ / __ / __

There were 674,000 victims of child abuse and neglect reported to child protective services in 2017.

▲
Department of Health and Human Services
▼

☐ Today I will report any neglect I observe or physical, sexual, or emotional abuse of a child to the police, local law enforcement, 911, or the National Domestic Violence Hotline at 1-800-799-SAFE (7233).

IT TAKES A VILLAGE TO RAISE A CHILD.

African proverb

☐ Today I will volunteer as a big brother or a big sister.

DATE: __ / __ / __

Community Service Day

**Do one of these important
services today. Check the box.**

☐ Read to a blind person.

☐ Walk a shelter dog.

☐ Shop for an elderly neighbor.

☐ Collect toys/toiletries for a

   homeless shelter.

☐ Donate used clothes or furniture.

☐ Support veterans or military

   families.

☐ Be an English-conversation

   partner.

☐ Donate blood.

☐ Prepare taxes as a volunteer.

☐ Teach healthy cooking.

☐ Deliver meals to shut-ins.

☐ Welcome a new neighbor.

☐ Thank a firefighter, police officer,

   or veteran.

☐ _____

          something else

The worst sin towards our fellow creatures is not to hate them, but to be indifferent to them.

George Bernard Shaw

Today, instead of walking past someone who was begging, I:

_____

_____

_____

_____

_____

_____

_____

A major study of bike helmet use around the world found that helmets reduce the risk of serious head injury by 70 percent.

The Guardian

Today I will:
- ☐ learn more about helmet requirements from the Bicycle Helmet Safety Institute (helmets.org)
- ☐ resolve to always wear a bike helmet
- ☐ wear visible clothing and reflective gear
- ☐ install a white front light and red back light on my bike

IF YOU GOT A HEAD, U NEED A HELMET!

Bike safety slogan

I've got a head and a helmet, so now I have to:

- [ ] travel in a bike lane, if possible
- [ ] make sure my shoelaces and pant legs don't get caught in the gear
- [ ] ride defensively
- [ ] learn my rights and responsibilities, which are the same as those of drivers

ONE WAY TO OPEN
YOUR EYES TO
UNNOTICED BEAUTY
IS TO ASK YOURSELF,
"WHAT IF I HAD
NEVER SEEN THIS
BEFORE? WHAT IF
I KNEW I WOULD
NEVER SEE IT AGAIN?"

Rachel Carson

DATE: __ / __ / __

WHAT IF I HAD NEVER SEEN _____ **BEFORE:**

_____

_____

_____

_____

_____

_____

DATE: __ / __ / __

WHAT IF I KNEW I WOULD NEVER SEE _____ **AGAIN:**

_____

_____

_____

_____

_____

_____

On any given night in 2018, about 553,000 people were homeless in the United States. About two-thirds were in emergency shelters or transitional housing programs. The rest were on the street, in abandoned buildings, or in other unsheltered places.

US Department of Housing and Urban Development

Today I will: ☐ volunteer at a homeless shelter

☐ contribute food or goods to a homeless shelter

DATE: __/__/__

PEOPLE WHO ARE HOMELESS ARE NOT SOCIAL INADEQUATES. THEY ARE PEOPLE WITHOUT HOUSES.

Sheila McKechnie

Today I:
- ☐ lobbied city officials for housing policies to ameliorate the homeless situation
- ☐ volunteered to help build or repair a home for people in need through an organization such as Habitat for Humanity

FOOD WASTE

Unused or spoiled food I threw away last week:

_____

_____

How I will shop differently this week:

_____

_____

Today's leftovers:

Breakfast: _____

Lunch: _____

Supper: _____

A dish I made with today's leftovers:

_____

_____

Rate yourself as a food-waste warrior (from 1 to 10, with 10 being the greatest): _____

DATE: __ / __ / __

Americans waste about a pound of food per person each day. Fruits and vegetables are the most likely to be thrown out, followed by dairy and meat.

The Guardian

☐ Today I learned how to compost food waste so that it can be used as fertilizer (epa.gov/recycle/composting-home).

DATE: __/__/__

Diarrheal disease is the second leading cause of death in children under five years old, killing **525,000** children every year, and is a leading cause of malnutrition.

World Health Organization

☐ Today I donated $10 for a packet of oral rehydration solution through WHO, UNICEF, or another world health organization.

DATE: __/__/__

DIARRHEAL DISEASE CAN BE PREVENTED THROUGH SAFE DRINKING WATER AND ADEQUATE SANITATION AND HYGIENE.

World Health Organization

Today I donated money to **CARE** or a similar organization for:

☐ a ceramic water filter ($30)

☐ 50 bars of soap ($25)

DATE: __ / __ / __

WHAT I THINK I CAN CHANGE LOCALLY:

_____

_____

_____

DATE: __ / __ / __

WHAT I THINK I CAN CHANGE GLOBALLY:

_____

_____

_____

DATE: __ / __ / __

AM I CRAZY?

_____

_____

_____

The people who are crazy enough to think they can change the world are the ones who do.

▲
Apple computer ad. 1997
▼

More people went hungry in 2017 than at any time in the previous decade. One out of nine people did not have enough to eat.

World Health Organization

☐ Today I joined or volunteered at an organization concerned with world hunger.

A DECENT PROVISION FOR THE POOR IS THE TRUE TEST OF CIVILIZATION.

Samuel Johnson

☐ I do enough for the poor.

☐ I do not do enough for the poor.

☐ **Today I will:**

_____

_____

_____

_____

DATE: __/__/__

HELPING HAND

Justine Lee and
Tria Chang, two young
professionals in San Francisco, were
upset by the extreme polarization during and after
the 2016 presidential election. Their solution is MADA
(Make America Dinner Again). This organization brings together
groups of six to eight people with different political views for respectful
conversation over a meal. Hosts get a guide, with some activities,
and can find their own guests or be matched up on the website
(makeamericadinneragain.com).

Lee and Chang's story inspired me to:

_____

_____

_____

_____

_____

_____

WE ARE JUST PEOPLE WITH OUR OWN STORIES AND REASONS FOR OUR BELIEFS. AT OUR CORE WE JUST WANT TO BE UNDERSTOOD.

Tria Chang

Today I will try to understand a different political belief from mine through:

☐ conversation with _____

☐ reading _____ .

Great works are performed not by strength, but perseverance.

Samuel Johnson

DATE: __ / __ / __

BY PERSEVERANCE I WAS ABLE TO ACCOMPLISH THIS IN MY COMMUNITY:

_____

_____

_____

_____

_____

_____

DATE: __ / __ / __

BY PERSEVERANCE I WAS ABLE TO ACCOMPLISH THIS NATIONALLY:

_____

_____

_____

_____

_____

_____

DATE: __ / __ / __

On International Women's Day,
I'm reflecting on the future
we all want for our daughters:
one where they can live out
their aspirations without limits.

Barack Obama

Today I: ☐ marked International Women's Day (March 8) on the calendar

☐ supported the aspirations of a young woman I know by:

_____

_____

_____

_____

_____

8 SIMPLE THINGS YOU CAN DO TO IMPROVE WOMEN'S RIGHTS

1) Raise your voice.

2) Support one another.

3) Share the workload.

4) Get involved.

5) Educate the next generation.

6) Know your rights.

7) Join the conversation.

8) Give to the cause.

UN Women

Today I supported a woman's rights by:

_____

_____

_____

_____

_____

ANIMAL WATCH

WHALE

Six of the 13 great whale species are classified as endangered. Yet Iceland and some other countries kill more than 1,000 whales a year, ignoring the international moratorium on commercial whaling. Whales also die from collisions with ships, entanglement in fishing nets, and corruption and disruption of their food supply due to water pollution and climate change.

☐ Today I explored the American Cetacean Society website (acsonline.org) to learn more about saving whales.

DATE: __ / __ / __

Leap! leap up, and lick the sky! I leap with thee; I burn with thee . . . defyingly I worship thee!

Herman Melville

☐ Today I wrote to the US Secretary of Commerce to support laws prohibiting whaling.

DATE: __ / __ / __

How much difference did you make for good after a year of doing one thing every day that changes the world?

Rate yourself from (1 to 10, with 10 being the greatest): _____

Compare your score with your rating at the beginning of the book:

_____

_____

_____

_____

Keep going!

GLOSSARY

carbon dioxide (CO_2)

A colorless, odorless greenhouse gas naturally produced when animals and people exhale air and when dead animals and plants decay. Carbon emissions from burning fossil fuels for energy, such as coal, oil, and natural gas, increase the concentration of carbon dioxide in the atmosphere.

GLOSSARY

carbon footprint

A measure of the impact our activities have on the environment, especially *climate change*, based on the total amount of greenhouse gases emitted each year by a person, family, or other unit.

carbon offset / carbon credit

Emissions savings or storage that can be considered to have canceled out carbon dioxide emissions that would have otherwise occurred. Individuals, companies, or governments may also pay to fund projects that generate energy from renewable sources, such as wind, solar, or biomass (fuel from animal and plant sources).

climate change

A significant change in the climate of a region over time. According to the UN Framework Convention on Climate Change, it is caused by higher levels of *greenhouse gases* in the atmosphere due to human activities as well as natural forces.

deforestation

The reduction of trees in a wood or forest due to natural forces or human activities such as burning or logging.

global warming

The gradual increase in temperature near the earth's surface, due to human activities that cause high levels of greenhouse gases to be released into the air.

greenhouse gases

Gases that tend to trap heat radiating from the earth's surface, causing warming in the lower atmosphere. The major greenhouse gases that cause climate change are carbon dioxide, methane, and nitrous oxide.

landfill

A site that is specially designed to dispose of solid waste on land.

sustainable development

Development using land or energy sources in a way that meets the needs of people today without reducing the ability of future generations to meet their needs.

Penguin Random House is committed to a sustainable future
for our business, our readers and our planet. This book is
made from Forest Stewardship Council® Mix certified paper.

ISBN 978-0-593-13507-5

Printed in China

Conceived and compiled by Dian G. Smith and Robie Rogge
Book and cover design by Nicole Block
Illustrations by Nicole Block

10 9 8 7 6 5 4 3 2 1

First Edition

The authors are donating 1 percent of their profits from this book
to organizations that improve the lives of people around the world
and the health of our planet.